Macramé Home Décor

LEISURE ARTS, INC. • Maumelle, Arkansas

CONTENTS

KNOTTING BASICS

BASIC SUPPLIES

- Ruler, yardstick, or tape measure
- Sharp scissors
- Craft glue
- Tape (masking, painter's, or washi)

TERMS

Cords – generic term for any fiber (jute, braided macramé cord, yarn, etc.) used to make the projects.

Filler Cord – generic term for any fiber or item (embroidery hoop, dowel, etc.) that the knots are worked over. It "fills" the knot.

KNOTS

Diagonal Double Half Hitch

Multiple cords are individually tied over a filler cord that has been laid diagonally across the working cords.

Follow **Figs. 1-6** to tie Diagonal Double Half Hitches with the cords indicated in the project instructions.

The figs show the knots tied to the right, but they can also be tied to the left.

Fig. 1

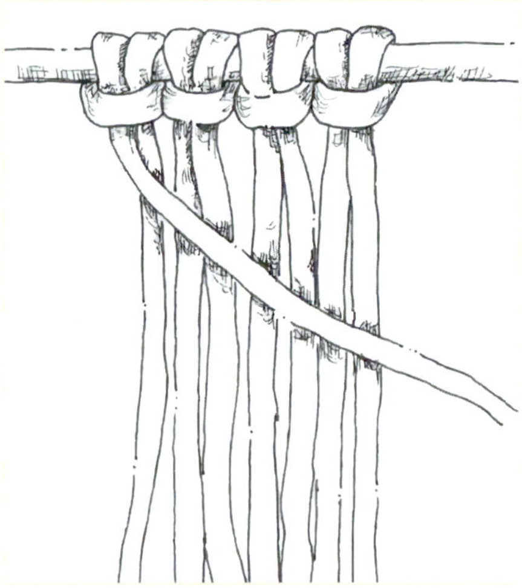

Fig. 2

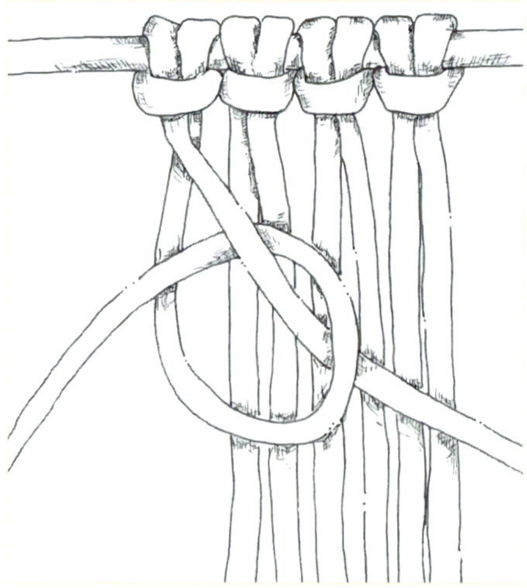

Fig. 3

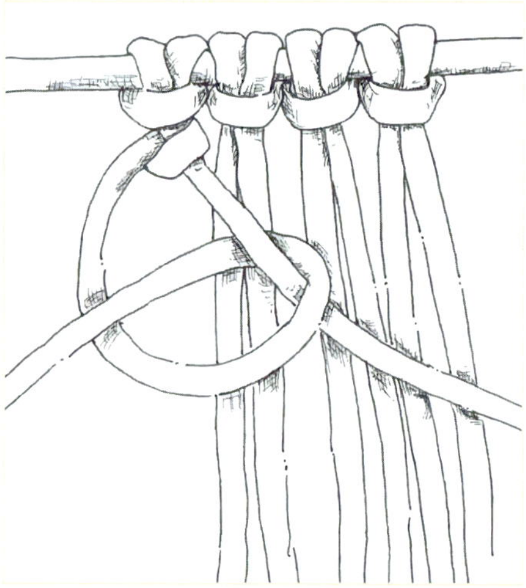

Fig. 4

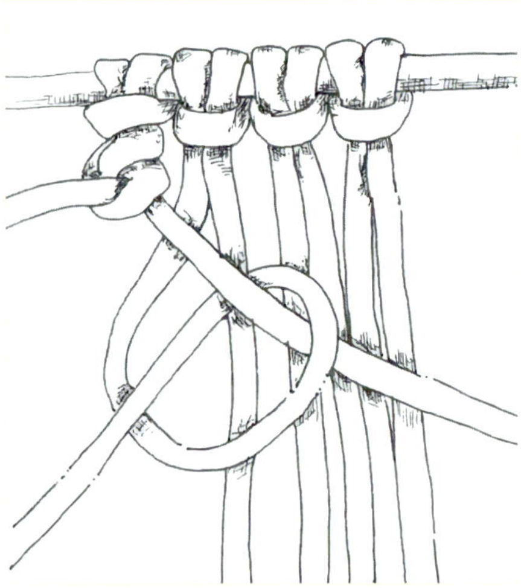

Fig. 5

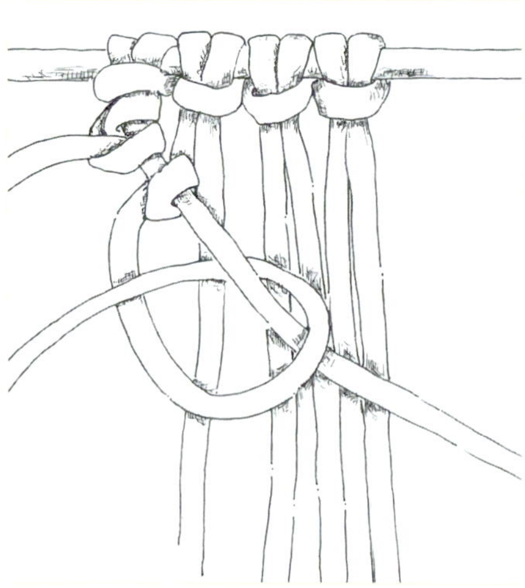

Fig. 6

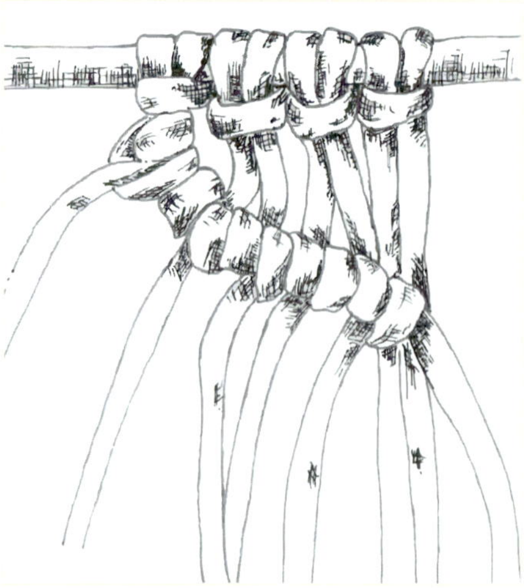

Horizontal Double Half Hitch

Multiple cords are individually tied over a filler cord that has been laid horizontally across the working cords.

Follow **Figs. 7-12** to tie Horizontal Double Half Hitches with the cords indicated in the project instructions.

Fig. 7

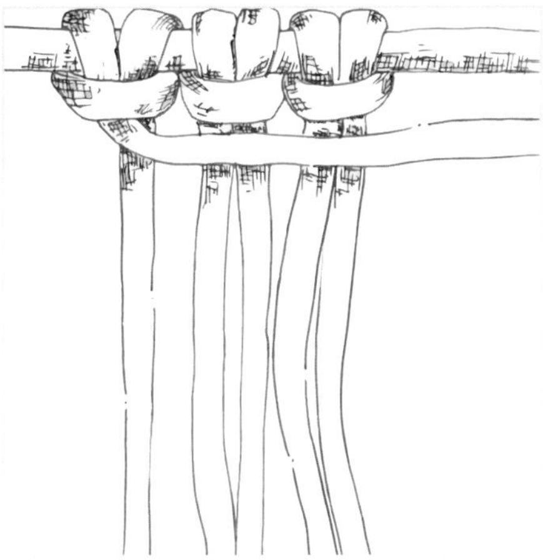

Fig. 8

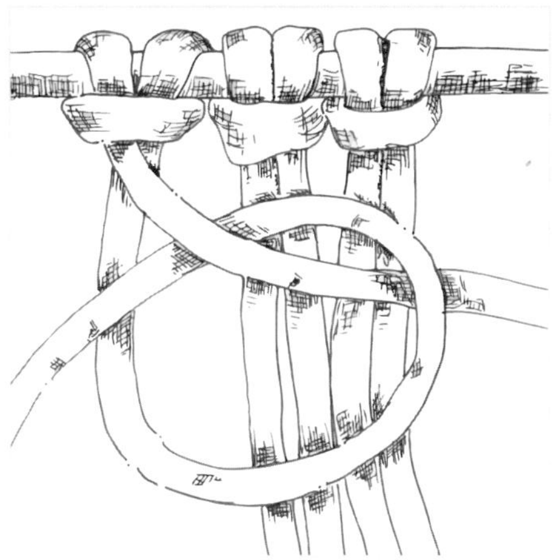

Fig. 9

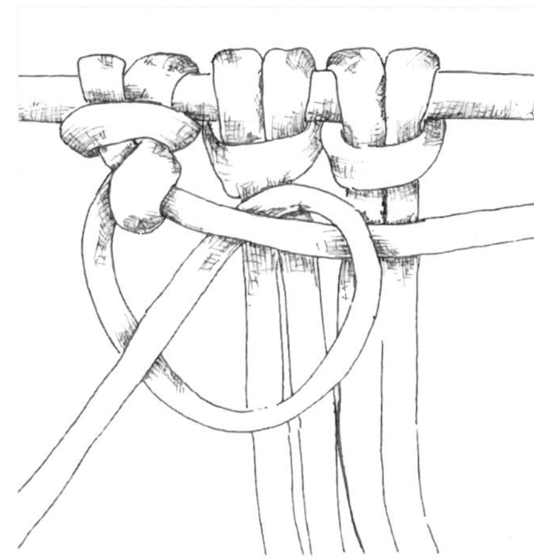

Fig. 10

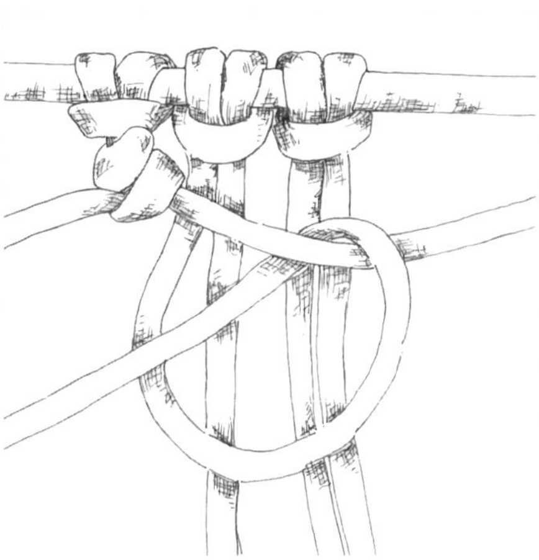

Fig. 11

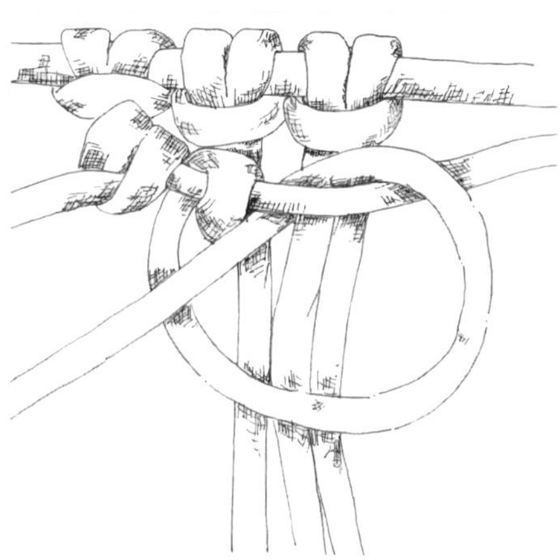

Fig. 12

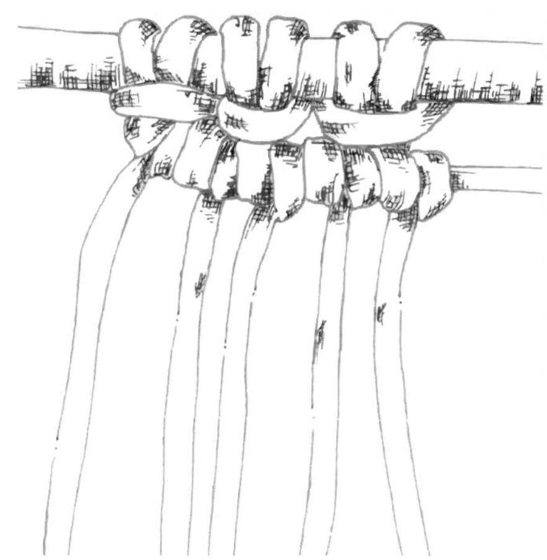

Lark's Head Knot

Lark's Head Knots are used to attach a cord or cords to an object such as another cord or dowel ***(Figs. 13-15)***.

Fig. 13

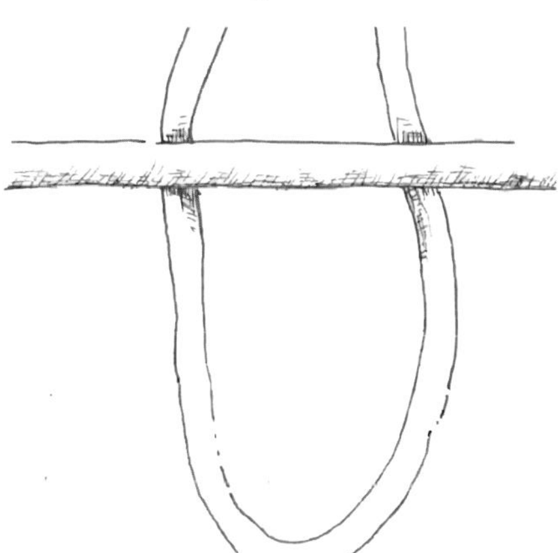

Fig. 14

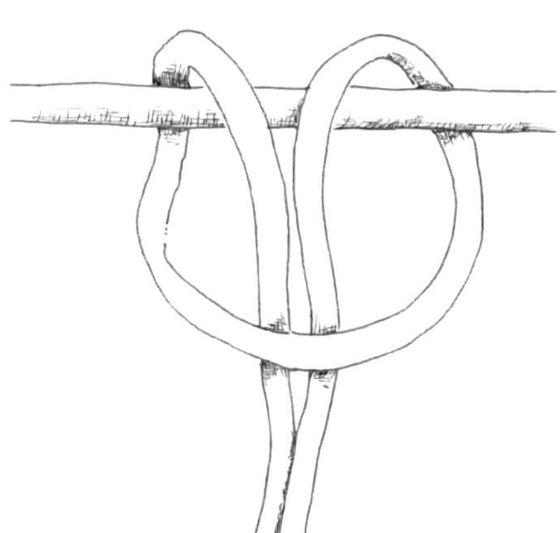

Fig. 15

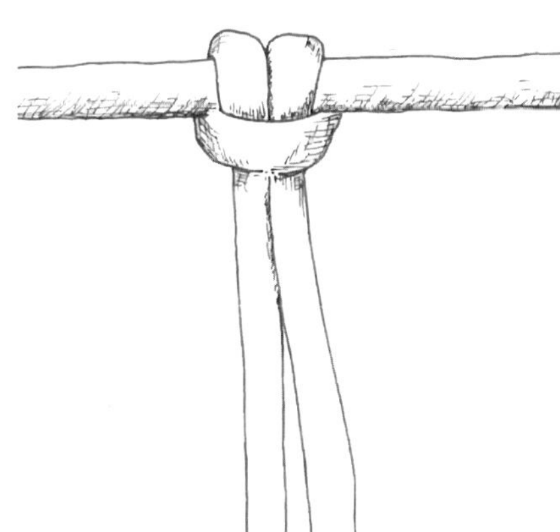

Overhand Knot

An Overhand Knot can be tied using a single cord or multiple cords ***(Figs. 16-17)***.

Fig. 16

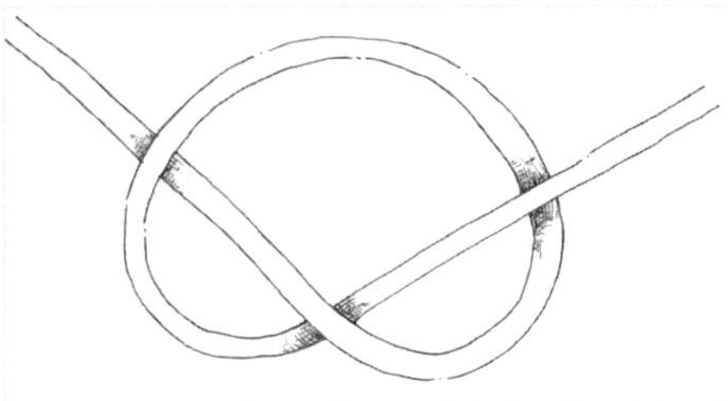

Fig. 17

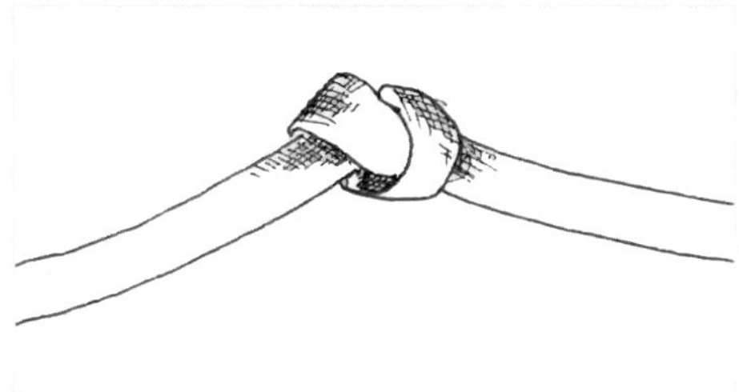

Square Knot

Follow **Figs. 18-19** to tie the first half of a Square Knot, pulling the cords to tighten.

Follow **Figs. 20-21** to tie the second half of a Square Knot, pulling the cords to tighten.

Fig. 18

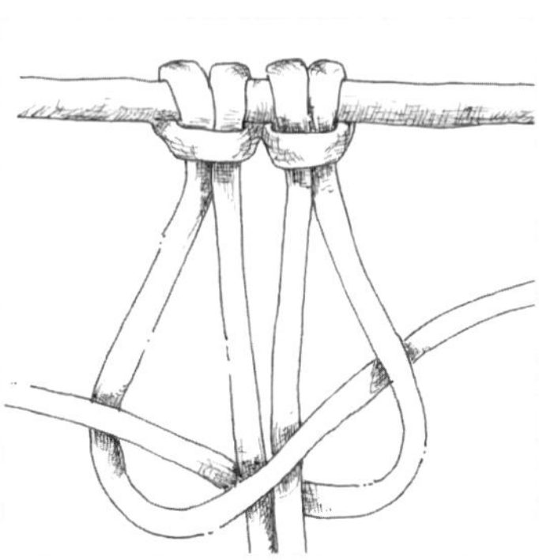

Fig. 19

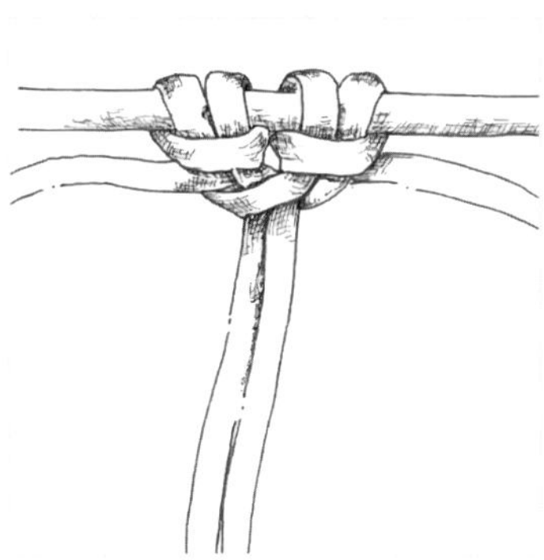

Fig. 20

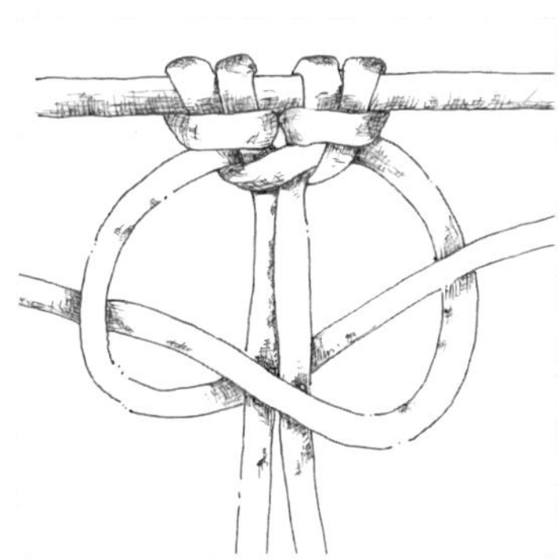

Fig. 21

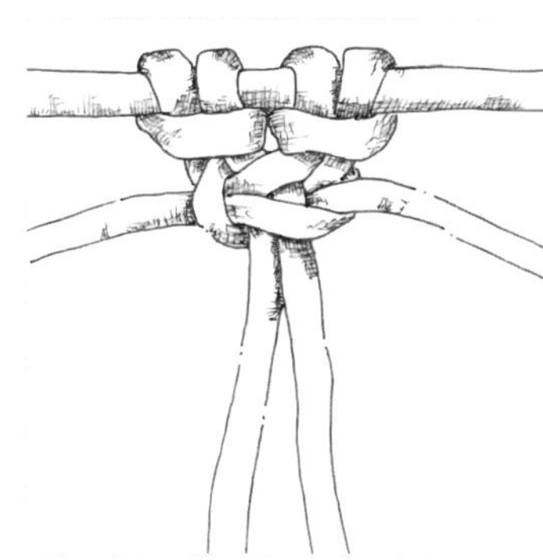

Half Square Knot

Follow **Figs. 18-19** above to tie the first half of a Square Knot, pulling the cords to tighten. Continue to tie the first half of a Square Knot, creating a spiral as seen in the Pom-Pom Wall Hanging on page 38.

Wrapped Knot

Form a loop with an 18" cord length. Wrap the cord around the filler cords 4-5 times. Bring the end through the loop ***(Fig. 22)***. Pull firmly on the opposite end of the cord until the loop disappears. Place a drop of glue on the knot. When the glue is dry, trim the cord ends ***(Fig. 23)***.

Fig. 22

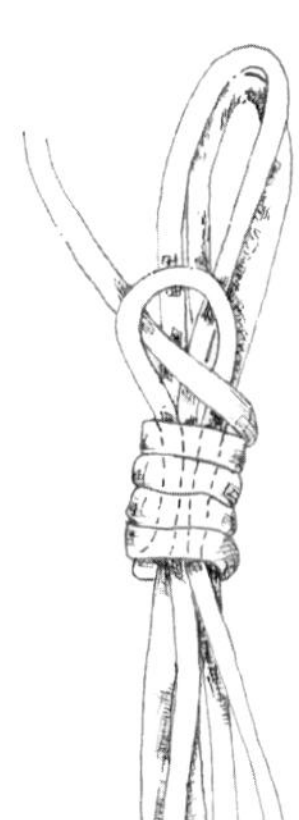

Fig. 23

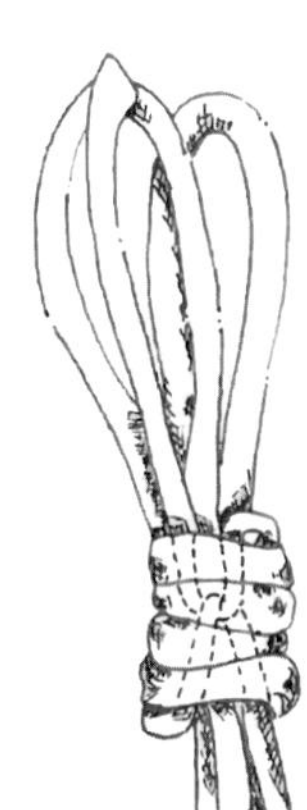

Home Décor

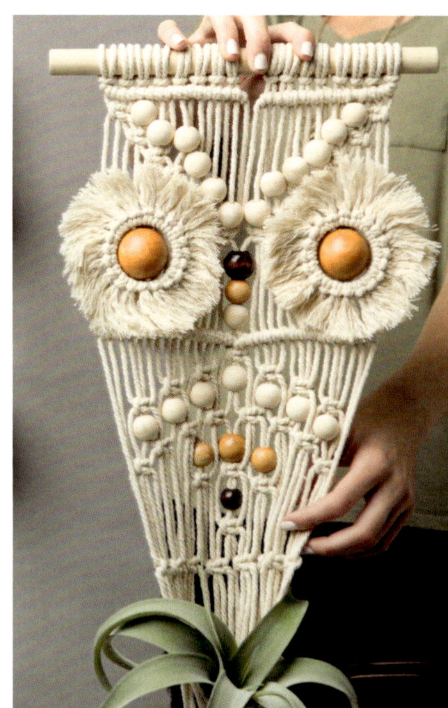

NOBODY'S FOOL

BOHO BANNER

I used a natural-colored 5mm cotton cord for this banner. The look can be changed by using thicker or thinner cord or a different color. Add charms, tassels, or pom-poms for even more fun - dream of the possibilities!

Design by Lisa Kettell
Finished Size: 88" x 6¾"

Materials

- ☐ 5mm cotton cord (about 11 yards per triangle; a total of 70 yards to make 6 triangles as shown)
- ☐ Large painted wood beads (be sure the cord will slide through the hole)
- ☐ Clipboard
- ☐ Scissors
- ☐ Tape measure
- ☐ Washi tape or masking tape

INSTRUCTIONS

1. Cut a 72" cord. For the first triangle, cut 10 36" cords. Tape the 72" cord to your work surface about 20" from one end. Leaving about 8"-10" slack, tape the opposite end of the cord to the work surface. Fold the 36" cords in half and use lark's head knots to attach them to the taped down cord.

2. Tie 5 square knots across the row.

3. Tape the first 2 cords and the last 2 cords to the work surface. Tie 4 square knots across the row.

4. Tape the next 2 cords on each side to the work surface. Tie 3 square knots across the row.

5. Tape the next 2 cords on each side to the work surface. Tie 2 square knots across the row.

6. Tape the next 2 cords on each side to the work surface. Tie the final square knot with the center cords. You should have a triangle shape.

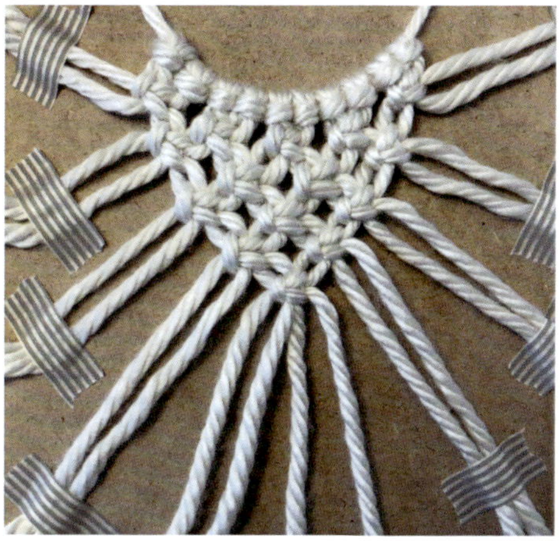

7. Starting on the right and working toward the center, tie double half hitch knots in a diagonal line until you reach the 9th cord. You will use the outermost right cord as the anchor or filling cord for all 10 knots.

8. Repeat the Step 7, this time starting on the left side and working toward the center until you reach the 10th cord. You will use the outermost left cord as the anchor cord for all 8 knots. Join the 2 center cords with a double half hitch knot. Trim the cords as desired and fray the ends. String a painted bead on the 72" base cord. Make 5 more triangles, stringing a painted bead between the triangles.

RAINBOW WALL HANGING

Make it large, make it small! While technically not macrame, these colorful creations are sure to bring a smile to all!

Design by Brook Berry, creator of BrooklynBerryDesigns.com
Finished Size: 9" x 7" (large); 3" x 2" (small)

Materials

- ☐ 10mm cotton rope (about 2⅝ yards for large rainbow and 1 yard for small rainbows)
- ☐ 18 gauge floral wire
- ☐ Yarn or embroidery floss in desired colors (6 for large rainbow and 3 for small rainbow)
- ☐ Masking tape
- ☐ Hot glue gun and glue sticks
- ☐ Hand sewing needle and thread

INSTRUCTIONS

1. For a large rainbow, cut 1 each: 12", 13", 14", 15½", 16½", and 18" rope lengths. Wrap the rope ends with masking tape to keep them from unraveling while you work.

2. Mark each rope about 2" from each end; use either a pen or another piece of tape. This indicates where you will start and stop the colored yarn or floss.

3. Cut a wire length that is the same length as the area between the inner markings or tape pieces for each rope length. This wire will be covered by the colored yarn or floss. Bend the wire into a gentle arch and temporarily tape the rope to the wire, making sure the wire is on the center portion of the rope.

4. Tie the yarn or floss to the rope at the marking and hold the tail in place. Begin wrapping the yarn or floss around the rope, covering the tail. Making sure the wire stays on the back of the piece, wrap the yarn or floss onto the rope until you reach the opposite marked side. Trim the yarn or floss and hot glue the end in place on the back.

5. Wrap the remaining ropes with yarn or floss, encasing the wire as you wrap.

6. Arrange the wrapped ropes in the desired color order and bend into the rainbow shape, adjusting the ropes to fit snugly against each other. Using a hand sewing needle and thread, sew the rainbow layers together from the back. For the hanger, form a loop from a scrap of wire and hot glue it to the rainbow back.

7. For the small rainbows, cut 2 each: 4", 4½", and 5" rope lengths. Wrap the rope ends with masking tape to keep them from unraveling while you work. Mark each rope about ¾" from each end; use either a pen or another piece of tape. Make each small rainbow in the same manner as the large rainbow.

PLACE MAT

After you tie the first set of knots creating 4 bundles, knotting is easier if you tape the top knots to your work surface.

Design by Angie Holden
Finished Size: 12" x 18"

Materials

- ☐ 2.5mm cotton rope cord (about 52 yards) cut into 32 54" lengths
- ☐ Scissors
- ☐ Tape measure
- ☐ Masking tape

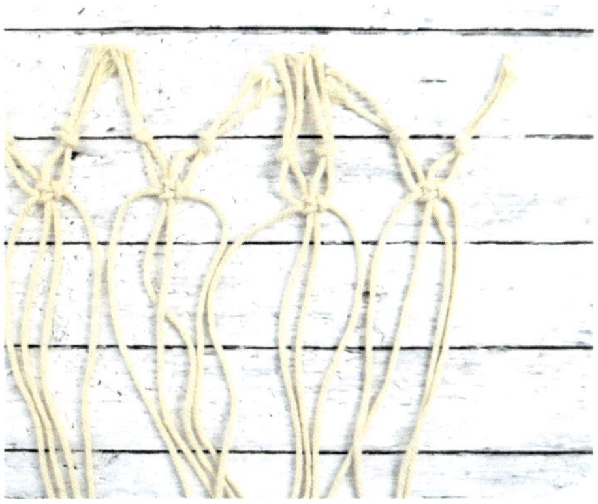

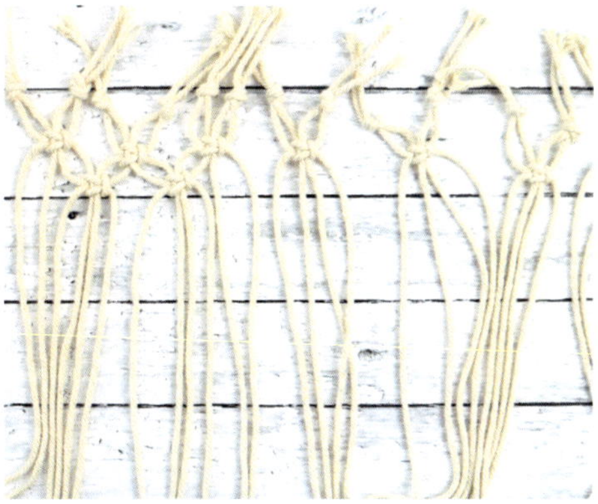

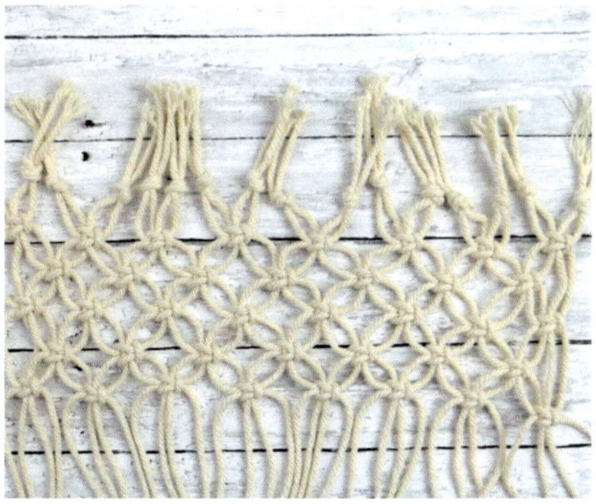

INSTRUCTIONS

1. Use overhand knots to tie 2 cords together about 2" from the ends. Repeat with remaining cords. Lay the bundles out on your work surface.

2. Tie two of these bundles together with a square knots about 1" below the overhand knots. Repeat to create 4 joined bundles.

3. Leaving the first two cords and last 2 cords unworked, work square knots across the project about 1" below the last row of knots.

4. Continue to tie rows of alternating square knots about 1" below the previous row until you have a total of 19 rows of knots.

5. To finish the place mat, knot the two cords on one end together using an overhand knot. Continue knotting two cords together across to the opposite end. Trim the cords to 2". Fray the cord ends if desired.

LAMPSHADE

There are a wide variety of shade frames available in lots of sizes and shapes. I used a 12" tall shade that was 6" square at the top and 16" square at the bottom. Use these instructions as a jumping off point if your shade is different.

Design by Debbie Murray and Shea Frogoso

For a frame that's 6" square on top, 16" square on bottom, and 12" tall

Materials

- ☐ Medium weight yarn that is on the thin side (I used 2 skeins of yarn that had 180 yards each)

  MEDIUM 4

- ☐ Super bulky yarn that has a metallic thread twisted in (I used 2 skeins of yarn that had 92 yards each)

  SUPER BULKY 6

- ☐ Metal lampshade frame
- ☐ Soft ribbon or rayon seam binding in a coordinating color (optional; I used 4 yards)
- ☐ Scissors
- ☐ Tape measure
- ☐ Size K (6.5mm) crochet hook

INSTRUCTIONS

1. Wrap all sections of the lampshade frame with the ribbon or seam binding. This step is optional but creates a nice finish for any area that will peek through after the knotting is finished.

2. Cut 80 lengths of the medium weight yarn, each measuring 6 times the height of the lampshade frame. Attach each cord to the frame with a lark's head knot.

Tip
If your lampshade frame is a smaller size, you may adjust the number of yarn lengths you cut, but be sure to keep them in multiples of 4.

3. Tie 5 rows of alternating square knots around the top of the frame, using 4 cords for each knot. As you turn the corner, tie the knot over the frame.

Note: *You'll work the same knotting patterns on all 4 sides of the frame.*

4. Tie the next row of square knots in an inverted "V" shape, tying two square knots in the center and dropping down about 1½" on the outer edges and evenly spacing the remaining knots.

5. Using the 2 cords closest to each side of the frame, tie 10-12 square knots down the edges of the frame until it aligns with the bottom of the "V" shape.

6. Starting at the center, tie 2 rows of double half hitch knots on each side, anchoring them by including the two cords from the sides.

7. Cut 32 lengths of medium weight yarn that are twice as long as the existing cord lengths. Use lark's head knots to attach 4 cords to each of the eight "corners" near the frame sides (see arrows on Photo below).

8. Tie 5 more rows of alternating square knots conforming to the frame shape and tying the corner knots over the frame.

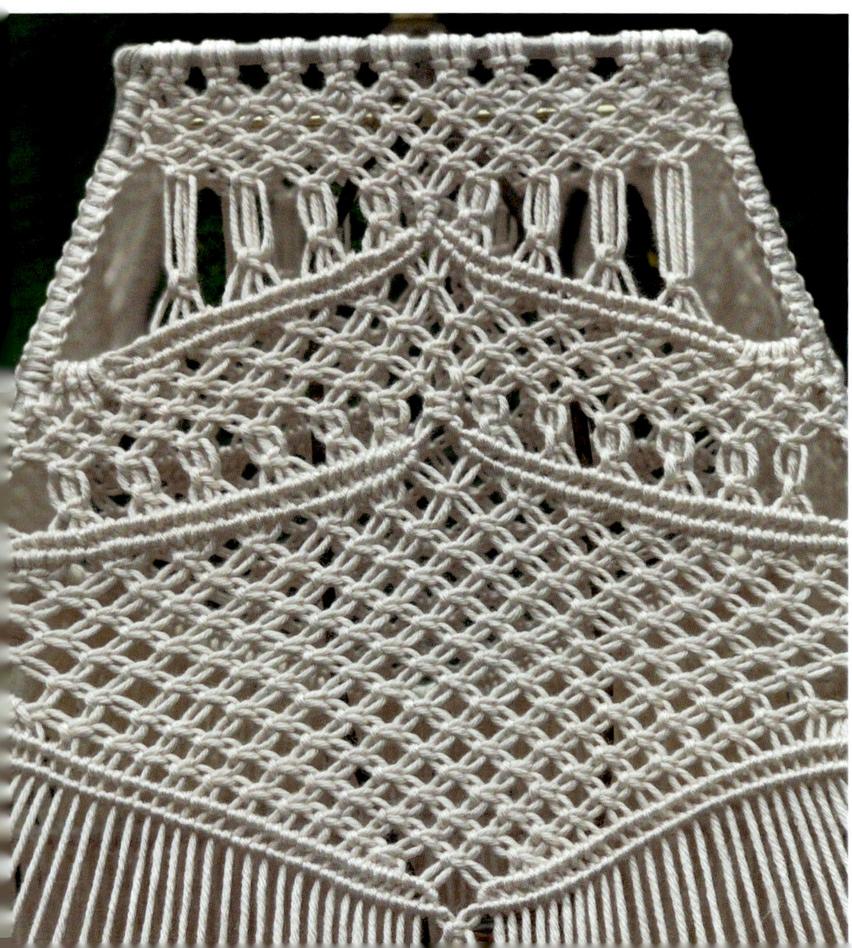

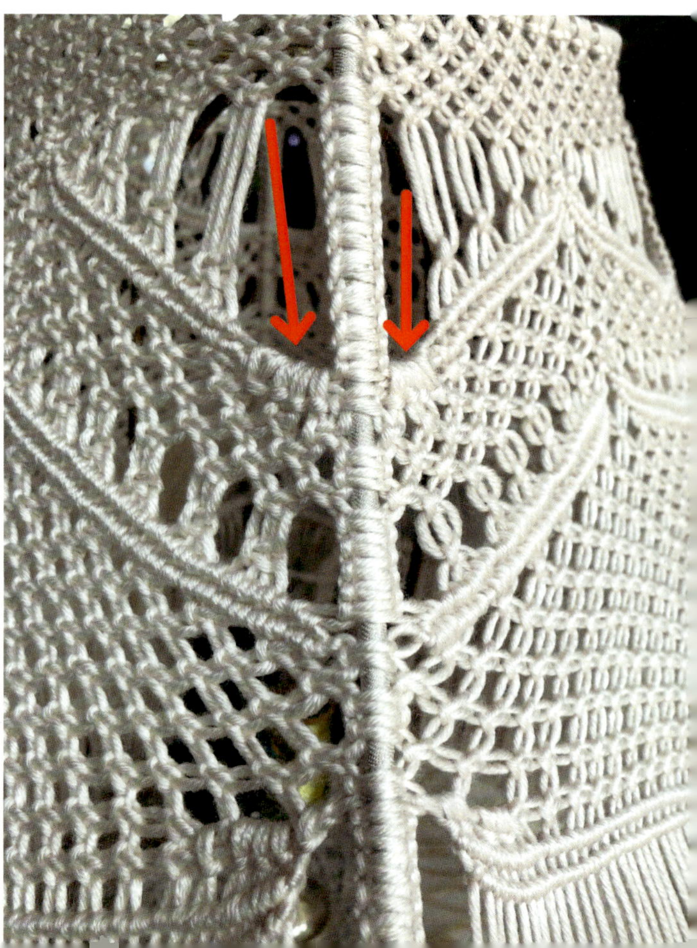

9. Tie the next row of square knots in an inverted "V" shape, tying two square knots in the center and dropping down about ½" on the outer edges and evenly spacing the remaining knots. Using the last 2 cords from each side, tie 4-6 square knots down the edges of the frame until it aligns with the bottom of the "V" shape.

10. Starting at the center, tie 2 more rows of double half hitch knots on each side, anchoring them by including the two cords from the sides.

11. Tie 5 rows of square knots, and then begin to decrease each row until there are 3 square knots across.

12. Cut 32 lengths of medium weight yarn that are twice as long as the existing cord lengths. Attach 4 cords to each of the eight sides as you did in Step 7.

13. Beginning at the sides with the new cords you added in Step 12, tie two rows of double half hitches in a "V" shape. Tie a square knot in the center.

14. Using the 2 cords closest to each side of the frame, tie square knots down the edges of the frame until you reach the frame bottom.

15. Tie all the cords on a side to the bottom edge of the frame with double half hitch knots. Cut 50-60 12" lengths of medium weight yarn. Use lark's head knots to attach these cords between the half hitch knots on 1 bottom edge of the frame. You'll want to cover the metal frame completely along the bottom edge. Repeat on the remaining 3 bottom edges. Leave the cords uneven for now.

Tip

Some of the original cords will still be very long, and you may be able to use the excess for these 12" pieces. You may want to cut these pieces as you work.

16. Cut 8 24" lengths of super bulky yarn. Fold each cord in half and use a square knot to attach 2 cords to each side of the frame adjacent to the last set of double half hitches. The ends will fall toward the center of each side.

17. Cut 15 20" lengths of super bulky yarn. Fold each cord in half and use a lark's head knot to attach the cord to one set of cord ends that were attached in Step 16. Repeat around the frame.

18. Gather the 2 sections on 1 side of the frame and use a square knot to secure the center cords in a gentle swag. Repeat around the frame. Trim the super bulky yarn ends as desired.

19. Trim the medium weight yarn ends to straighten. Gently separate the bulky weight yarn lengths to create a "curly" effect.

20. Cut 16 24" lengths of super bulky weight yarn. Holding 2 cords together, fold the cords in half and use a square knot to attach 4 cords to each side of the frame just below the first 5 rows of square knots near the frame top.

21. Weave the cords under and back out through the knotted side. Use the 2 outermost cords to tie 2 square knots around the other 6 cords, forming a tassel. Separate the yarn lengths to create curly fringe. Trim the ends as desired.

22. Cut 80 4½" lengths of super bulky yarn. Use a lark's head knot to attach each cord to the frame top, placing them between the existing lark's head knots. A crochet hook makes it easier to get in between the tight spaces. Trim the yarn to about 1¼". Separate the yarn lengths to create curly fringe.

HEARTS WALL HANGING

I dyed the cords for the heart center and tassel a rose color. I lightly painted diluted dye on some of the other cords. My photos show some cords that were not left in the dye for very long for a more ombré appearance.

Design by Olga Boccagno
Finished Size: 19" x 27"

Materials

- ☐ ½" diameter wood dowel (19" long)
- ☐ 3mm cotton cord (about 110 yards)
- ☐ Fabric dye for cotton fabrics
- ☐ Scissors
- ☐ Tape measure

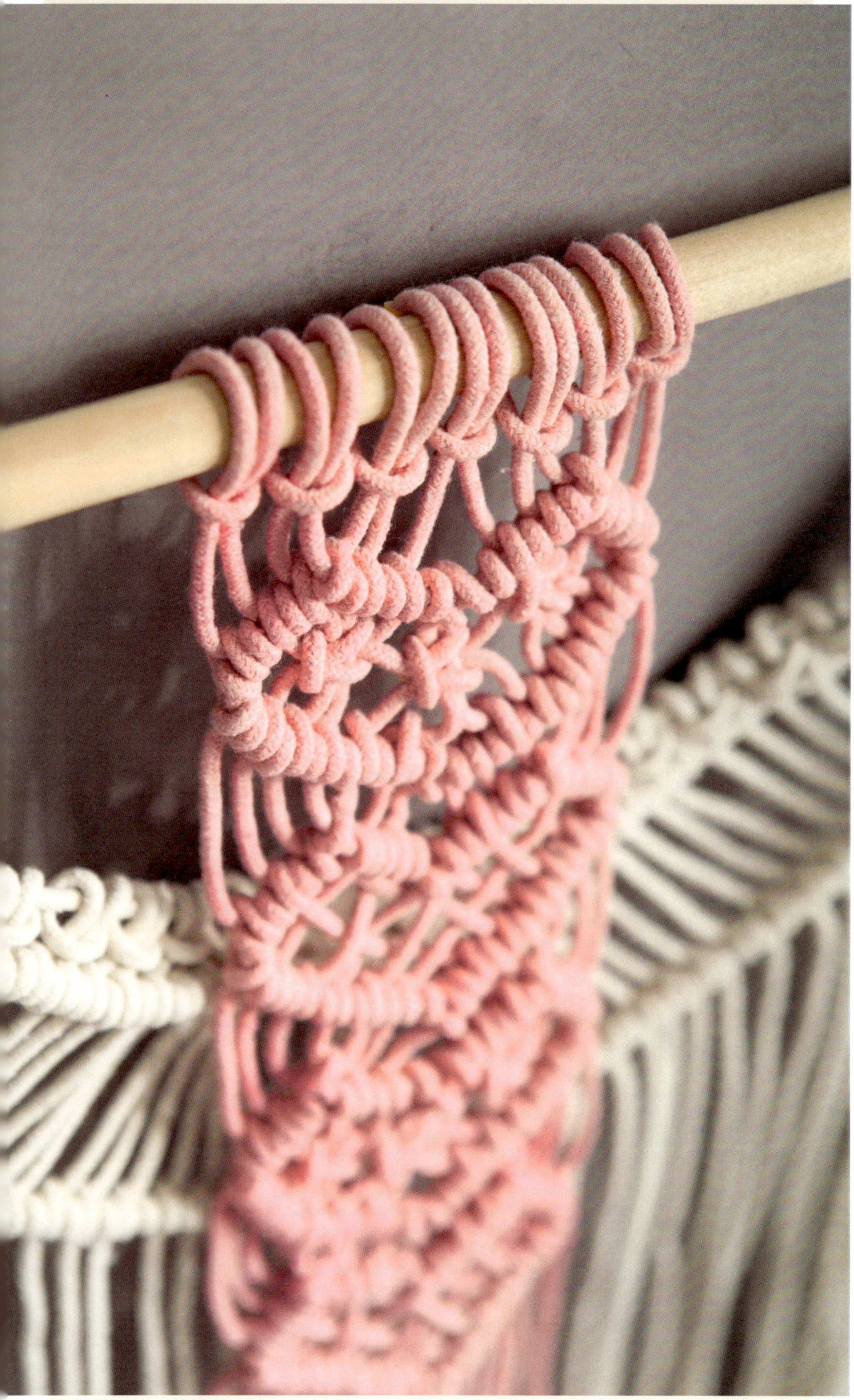

INSTRUCTIONS

1. Cut 7 12 foot cords and 10 24" cords. Follow the manufacturer's instructions to dye the cords. Let dry completely. Set the 24" cords aside until Step 18.

2. Use lark's head knots to attach the 7 12 foot cords to the dowel.

3. Starting on the left and using cord 4 as the anchor cord, tie 4 double half hitch knots diagonally starting about 1" below the dowel. Repeat on the right side. Tie a double half hitch at the center.

4. Take cord 4 to the left and using it as the anchor cord, tie 3 double half hitch knots diagonally. Take the anchor cord toward the right and tie 1 double half hitch. Repeat on the right side.

5. Make a square knot with cords 3-6 and 9-12. Make another square knot in the middle with cords 6-9.

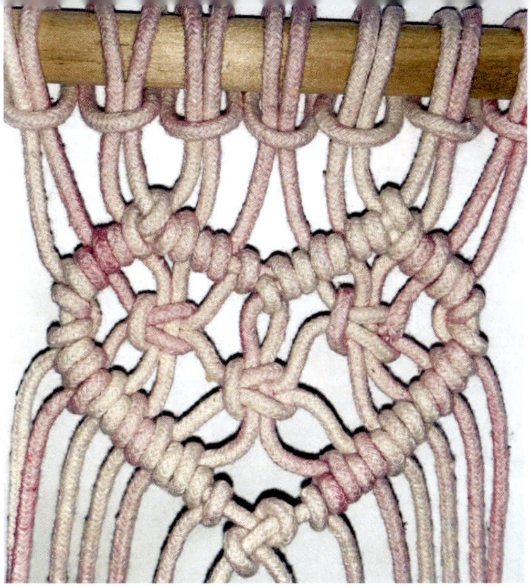

6. Take cord 2 to the right and tie 5 double half hitch knots diagonally. Repeat with cord 13, taking the cord to the left. Tie a double half hitch at the center to join and complete the first heart.

7. Step down 1" and make the top of the next heart following Steps 3-6, omitting Step 5 and crisscrossing the cords instead of tying square knots.

8. Repeat Steps 2-7 to complete a total of 4 hearts.

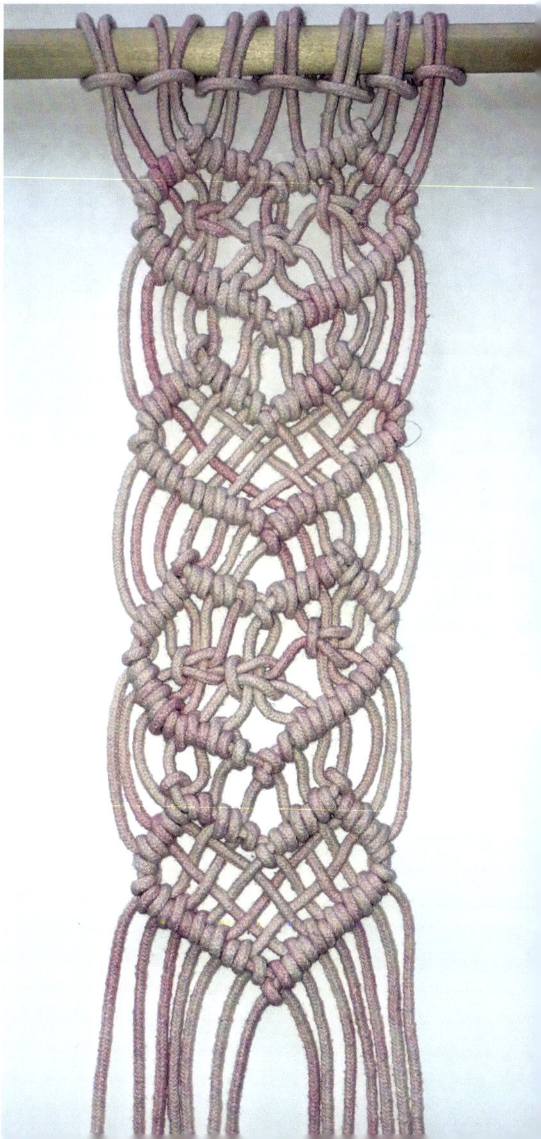

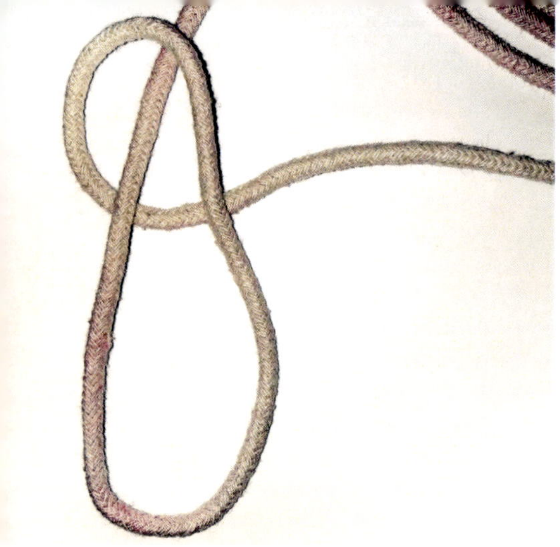

9. The cord ends on the hearts are finished with barrel knots. For each center cord, fold the cord about 11½" below the bottom heart. Wrap the end around the cord about 1½" above the fold.

10. Wrap the cord 7-8 times. Pull the end through the loop at the bottom.

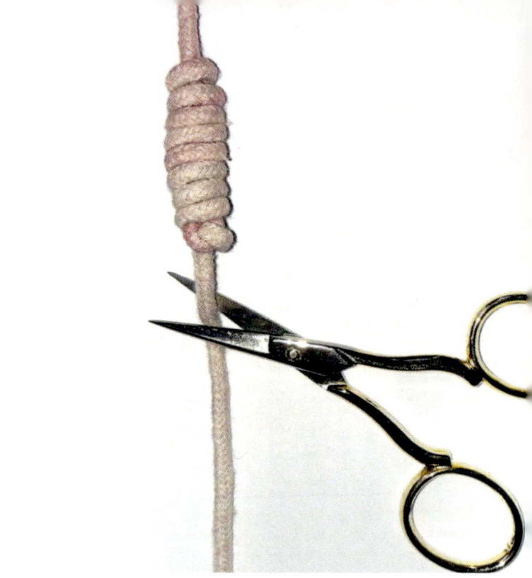

11. Tighten the knot and trim the excess cord. Continue to finish the cord ends with barrel knots, making them shorter as you work toward the ends.

12. Now we will make the background part of the wall hanging. Attach an 18 foot cord to the dowel with lark's head knots about 18" apart on the dowel. Allow the middle part of the cord to sag about 5" below the dowel.

13. Cut 26 6 foot cords. Use lark's head knots to attach the cords to the center swag you just put on the dowel.

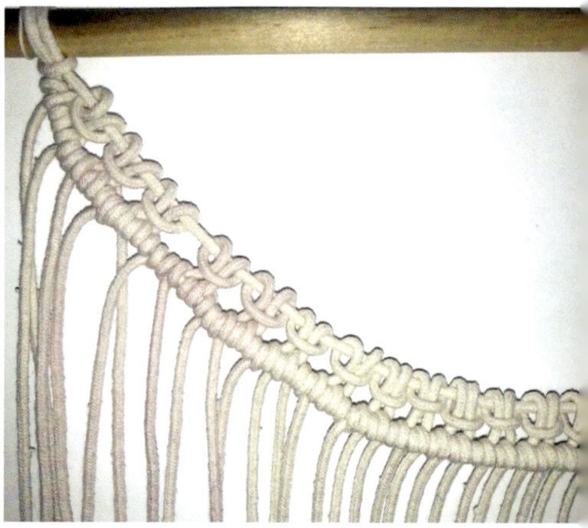

14. Starting on the left and using the outermost cord as the anchor cord, tie 26 double half hitch knots; be sure to follow the curve of the swag and place the double half hitch knots right below the lark's head knots. Alternate regular double half hitch knots and double half hitch knots with an extra loop on one side.

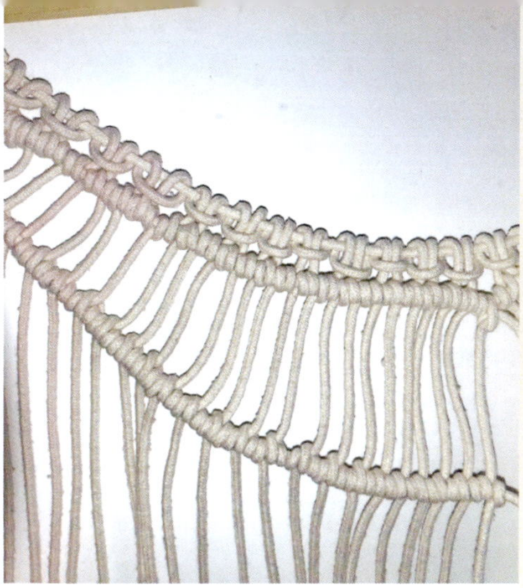

15. Repeat Step 14 with the outermost right cord and tying toward the center. Tie a double half hitch knot with the 2 center cords.

16. Starting on the left and using the outermost cord as the anchor cord, tie 26 double half hitch knots. The knots should start close to the previous row of double half hitch knots and gradually increase to about 3" away from the previous row.

17. Repeat Step 16 with the outermost right cord and tying toward the center. Tie a double half hitch knot with the 2 center cords. Repeat Step 9-11 to finish the ends with barrel knots.

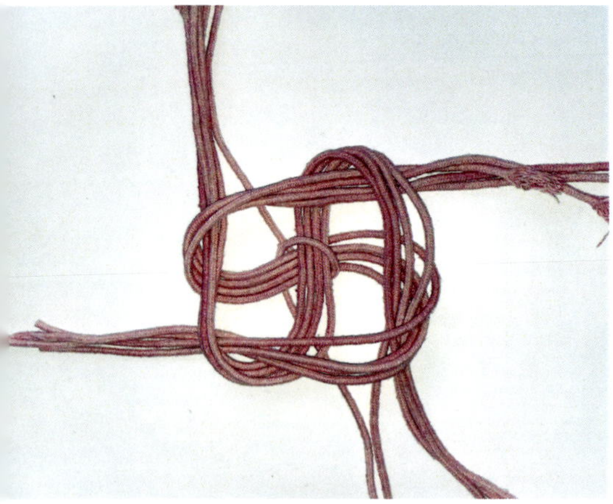

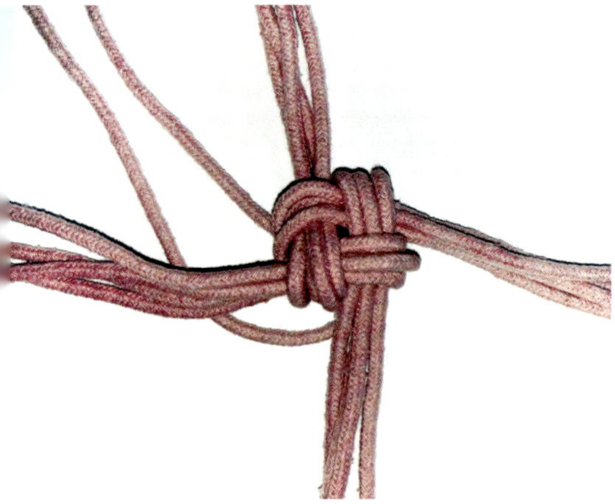

18. For the tassel, cut 8 24" cords and a 30" cord. Place 4 of the shorter cords on the work surface. Place the remaining 4 shorter cords across the first 4. Wrap the longer cord around the center crossed area.

19. Make a cross knot with the criss-crossed cords.

20. Pull the ends to tighten and adjust the knot. Make another cross knot on top of the first one.

21. Gather the cords and secure them with a wrapped knot, using a 24" cord to wrap. Trim the cords as desired and tie an overhand knot at the end of each cord. Use the loose cord ends at the tassel top to hang the tassel on the dowel. Tie a 32" cord to the dowel ends for a hanger.

OWL PLANT HANGER

You may attach a cord at the top of your project to hang it from, or hang it by the dowel from a hook in the wall.

Design by Kaleen Lounsbury
Finished Size: 11" x 44"

Materials

- ☐ 12" wooden dowel or metal pipe
- ☐ 4mm cotton cord (about 85 yards)
  - 16 14' lengths
  - 40 6" lengths for eyes
  - 3' length for gathering knot
- ☐ Thin string to attach eyes
  2 12" lengths
- ☐ 26 beads in assorted sizes & colors
- ☐ 2 2" diameter metal rings for eyes
- ☐ 2 1½" diameter beads for eyes
- ☐ Scissors
- ☐ Tape measure
- ☐ Masking tape
- ☐ Pet slicker brush or fine-tooth comb

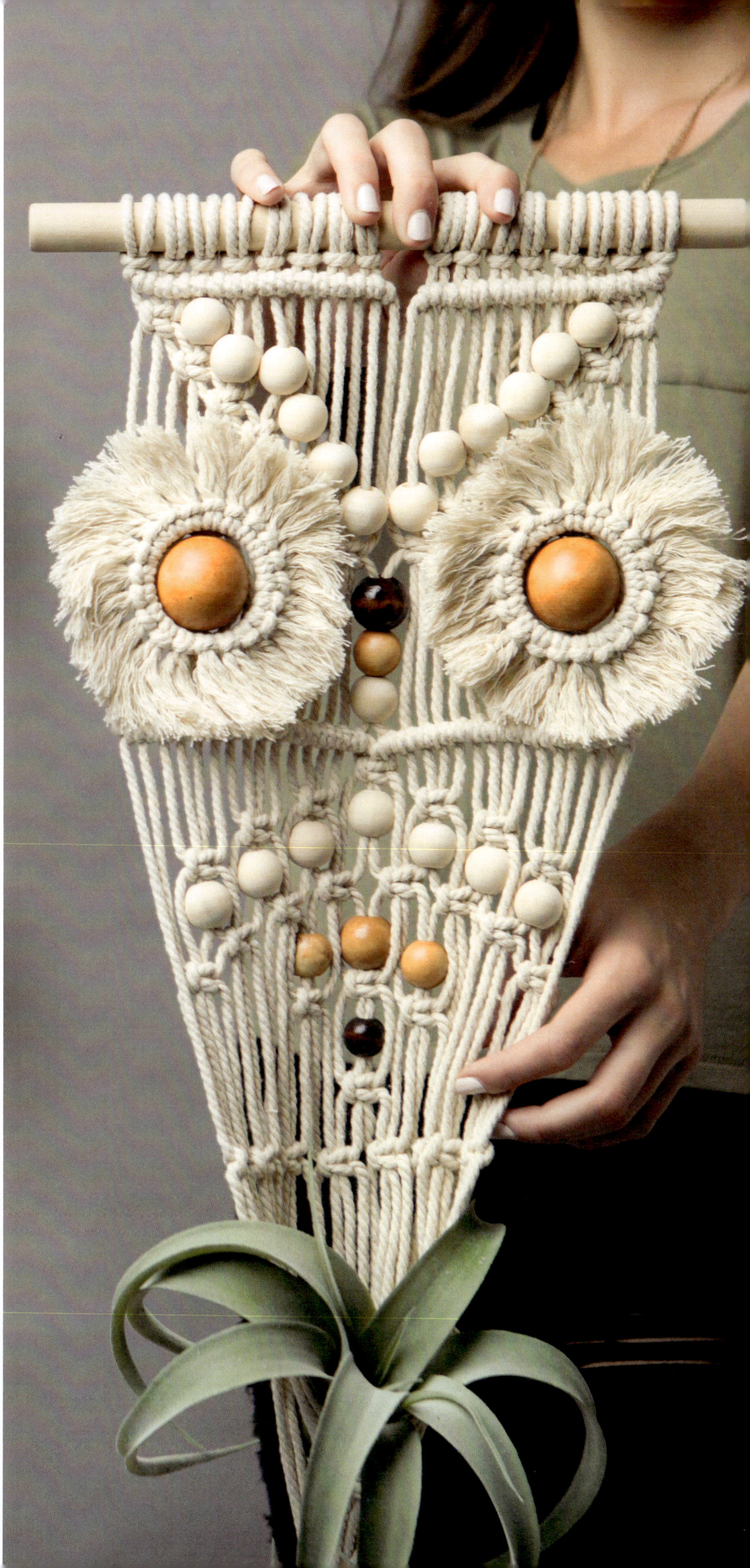

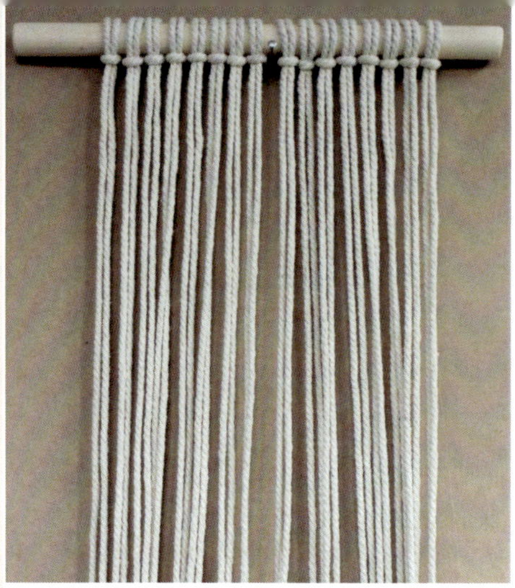

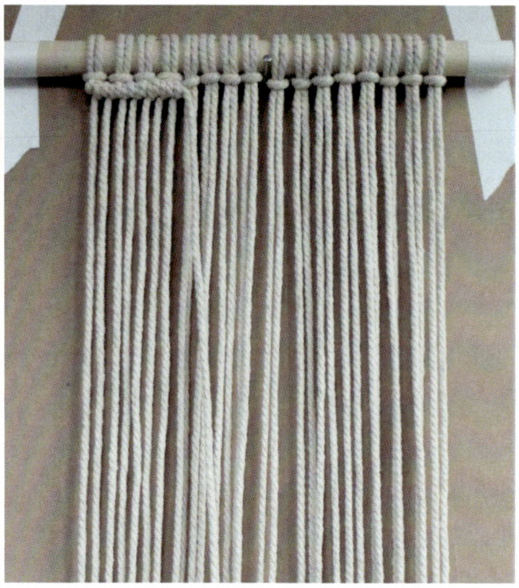

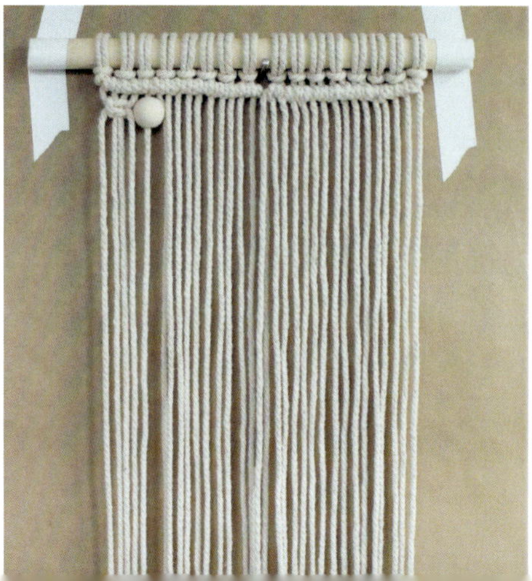

INSTRUCTIONS

1. Use lark's head knots to join the 14' lengths to the dowel. Tape the dowel to your work surface.

2. Starting on the left and working toward the center, tie double half hitch knots in a straight horizontal line until you reach the 17th cord. You will use the outermost left cord as the anchor or filling cord for all 15 knots.

3. Repeat the previous step, this time starting on the right side and working toward the center until you reach the 16th cord. You will use the outermost right cord as the anchor or filling cord for all 15 knots.

4. Now you will begin making the "V" shape of your owl. Using the 4 outermost cords on the left side, tie a square knot. String a bead on the 5th cord.

5. Tie the next square knot using the right 2 cords of the previous square knot and the next 2 cords closest to them on the right. String a bead on the 7th cord. Make a third square knot using the right 2 cords of the previous square knot and the next 2 cords closest to them on the right. The square knots should rest loosely beneath the beads, descending down to begin to form a "V" shape.

6. Repeat this pattern until you have reached the 16th cord from the left side of the project. Beads will be strung on the 5th, 7th, 9th, 11th, 13th, and 15th cords.

7. Now you will create the right side of the "V" shape. Again, starting with the 4 outermost cords, start the square knots. Each following square knot will take 2 cords from the previous square knot and the 2 cords closest to those on the left side this time. Once you have reached the middle, you should have 2 beads meeting at the bottom of your "V" shape.

8. String 3 beads on the 2 very middle cords. This creates the owl's beak.

9. To create the owl's eyes, tie a square knot using the 4th through the 7th cords. Repeat with the 26th through the 29th cords. The knots for the owl's eyes should be level with the bottom 2 beads of the "V" shape.

10. String a large bead on the 5th and 6th cords. Tie a square knot under the bead. String a large bead on the 27th and 28th cords. Tie a square knot under the bead.

11. Using the left outermost cord as the anchor or filling cord, tie double half hitch knots in a straight horizontal line until you reach the 17th cord.

12. Repeat Step 11 on the right side of the project with the very outermost right cord as the anchor or filling cord and working toward the center until you reach the 16th cord.

13. Using the 4 cords in the very center, tie a square knot. String a bead on the middle 2 cords of that square knot.

14. Working out from the middle, create descending square knots using the 4 cords adjacent to the previous square knot. String a bead below each of these square knots.

15. Now we will do a series of square knots beneath the beads. For the first one, use the left cord from the center bead and the 3 adjacent cords to the left. The remaining square knots on the left side will follow the same pattern, taking the left cord from the bead above and the 3 adjacent cords to the left. Repeat this process, stopping when you have 1 unworked cord on the left side.

16. Repeat Step 15 on the right side.

17. String a bead on the 2 middle cords. Skip 2 cords on either side and string a bead on the next 2 cords, positioning the 2 outer beads slightly lower than the middle bead. Tie a square knot beneath each bead.

18. String the last bead on the 2 middle cords. Tie a square knot beneath the bead.

19. Tie a straight row of square knots, starting on the left side of the project about ¾" below the last bead.

20. Tie a square knot using the 3rd through 6th cords on the left side, about 2" below the previous row of square knots. Tie another square knot using the next four cords to the right. Repeat on the right side with the 23rd through 26th cords and the 27th through 30th cords.

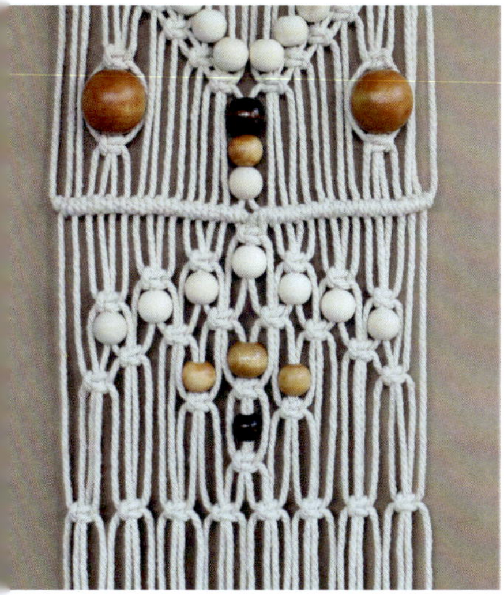

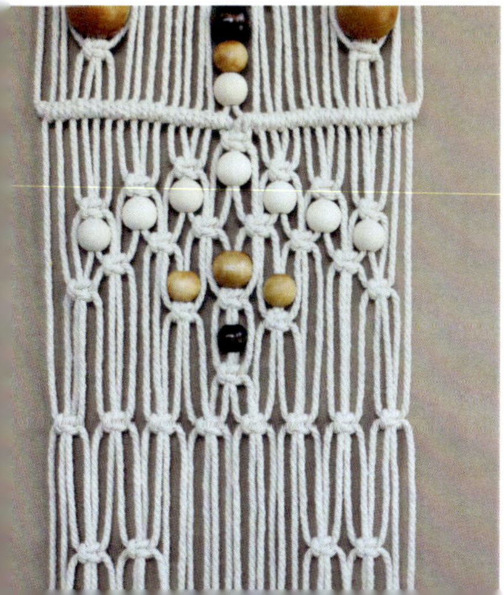

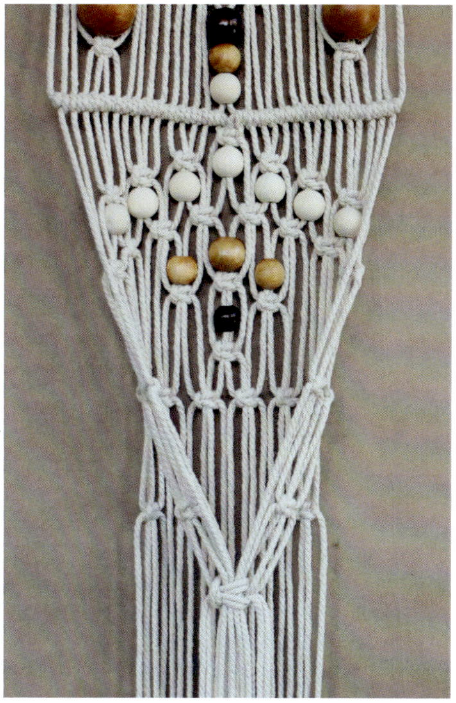

21. Gather the 6 outermost cords from the left side and the 6 outermost cords from the right side of the project. Tie a square knot using the 8 outermost of those 12 as the filler for the square knot and the remaining 4 as the working cords for the knot. This large square knot should rest about 1½" below the previous square knots.

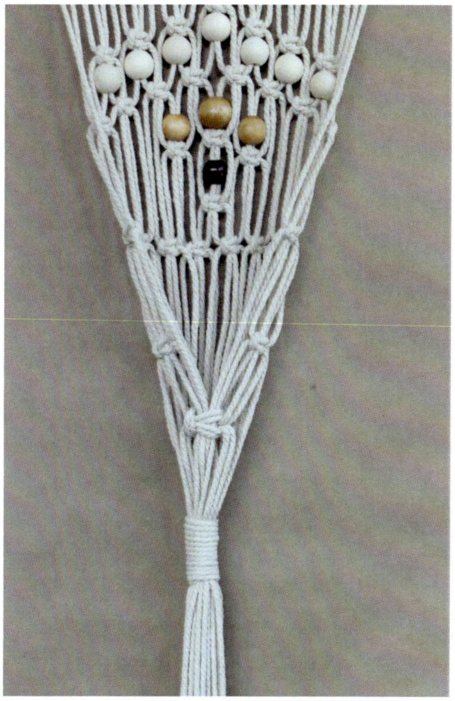

22. Gather all cords 1½" below square knot and tie together with a wrapped knot. Unwind the cords or comb out to desired fluffiness with the slicker brush or fine-tooth comb. Trim to the desired length.

23. For the owl's eyes, use lark's head knots to join 20 6" cords to each metal ring, securing a thin string behind one knot on each ring.

24. Comb out the cord ends using the slicker brush or fine-tooth comb. Trim to the desired length.

25. Use the thin string to tie the eye rings over the 2 large beads. A simple knot is fine to join these to the project!

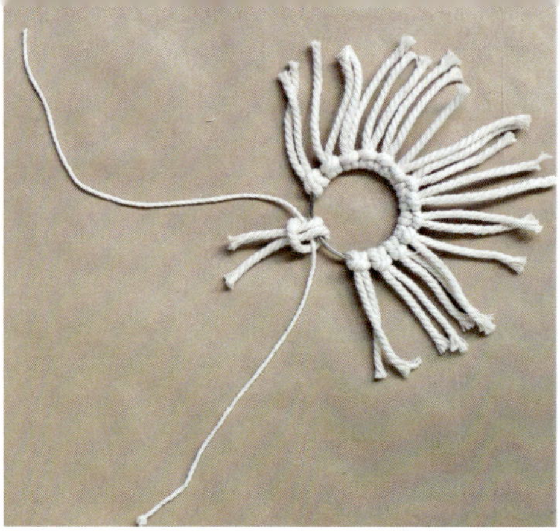

POM-POM WALL HANGING

Explore texture and color with this wall hanging. I used a variety of colors and thicknesses of yarns for the pom-poms. The tones and shades of white are perfect in today's modern home!

Design by Lynda Kanase
Finished Size: 12" x 40"

Materials

- ☐ Yarn A - Jumbo tubular snow white yarn – 77 yards (I used Bernat® Maker Big™ yarn in Snow)
- ☐ Yarn B - Super Bulky cream yarn – 160 yards (I used Bernat® Beyond™ yarn in Cream)
- ☐ Additional white/cream yarn for pom-poms
- ☐ 12" diameter wooden embroidery hoop (inner ring only)
- ☐ Pom-pom makers in various sizes
- ☐ Darning needle
- ☐ Rubber bands
- ☐ Scissors
- ☐ Tape measure

INSTRUCTIONS

1. Cut 8 26-foot cords from the jumbo yarn (A). Fold each cord in half and loosely wrap the ends into a bundle; secure with a rubber band. This is prevent the cords from dragging on the ground as you work.

2. Cut 8 28-foot cords from the super bulky yarn (B). Fold each cord in half and loosely wrap the ends into a bundle; secure with a rubber band.

3. Use a lark's head knot to secure each cord to the inner ring of the embroidery hoop. Attach the cords in the following order: B, B, A, B, B, A, B, A, A, A, A, A, B, A, B, B

4. Skipping the first 2 B and last 2 B cords, tie a row of 7 square knots right below the wood ring.

5. Tie a row of 8 square knots below the previous row.

6. Repeat Steps 4 and 5 to create 4 rows of alternating square knots.

7. Use the first 4 B cords to tie 20 half square knots. Tie 6 square knots across the next 24 cords. Use the last 4 B cords to tie 20 half square knots.

8. Skipping the first 2 and last 2 A cords, tie a row of 5 square knots.

9. Use the first 2 A and the next 2 B cords to tie 14 half square knots. Tie 4 square knots across the next 16 cords. Use the last 2 B and 2 A cords to tie 14 half square knots.

10. Skipping the first 2 B and the last 2 A cords, tie a row of 3 square knots.

11. Use the first 2 B and the next 2 A cords to tie 12 half square knots. Tie 2 square knots across the next 8 cords. Use the last 4 A cords to tie 8 half square knots.

12. Tie a row of 2 square knots.

13. Use the first 2 B and the next 2 A cords to tie 11 half square knots. Use the last 4 A cords to tie 8 half square knots.

14. You should now have 8 columns of half knots. Tie a square knot connecting columns 1 and 2 (use cords 3B, 4B, 5A, and 6A). Tie a square knot connecting columns 7 and 8 (use cords 27A, 28A, 29B, and 30B).

15. Use cords 1B-4B to tie a square knot. Use cords 29B-32B to tie a square knot.

16. Repeat Step 14 to connect columns 2 and 3 (cords 7B, 8B, 9B, and 10B) and columns 6 and 7 (cords 23A, 24A, 25B, and 26B).

17. Use cords 5A, 6A, 7B, and 8B to tie a square knot. Use cords 25B, 26B, 27A, and 28A to tie a square knot.

18. Using cords from adjacent columns, connect columns 3 and 4, columns 4 and 5, and columns 5 and 6.

19. Tie a row of 4 square knots right below the previous row. Tie one final square knot using the center 4 cords (2 B's and 2 A's).

20. Trim cord ends to about 17", angling as desired. Save the trimmings to make pom-poms.

21. To make a tasselled cord, cut a 30" cord of B. Cut 2 20" cords of B and 12 10" cords of B. Fold 6 10" cords in half and tie them to one end of the 30" cord. Align one end of the 20" cord with the bottom of the tassel and tightly wrap the top part of the tassel. Using a darning needle, run the remaining cord end behind the wrapped section. Trim all ends even. Use the remaining 10" and 20" cords to add a tassel to the remaining end of the 30" cord.

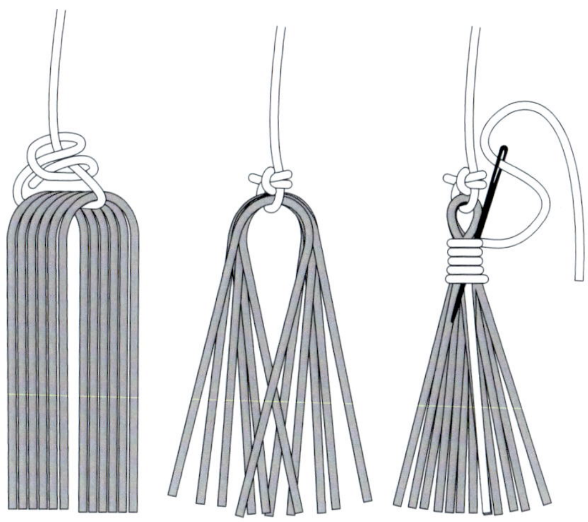

22. Repeat Step 21 with another 30" cord. Repeat Step 21 with 2 23" cords.

23. Use lark's head knots to attach the 30" cords to the wood ring on either side of the wall hanging. Attach the 23" cords next to the 30" cords. Adjust the tassels to cascade from short on the outside to long on the inside on both sides.

24. Follow manufacturer's instructions to make 3 large (about 3"), 5 medium (about 2¼"), and 4 small (about 1½") pom-poms. Tie the pom-poms on the wood ring.

Fashion Accessories

CROSSBODY BAG

This cute and functional bag only looks complicated. Alternating square knots come together in a chevron pattern to form each side of the bag. Dowels and end caps give the bag structure.

Design by Alexis Middleton
Finished Size: 20" long (including fringe, but not straps) with a 9" wide top opening

Materials

- ☐ 4.5mm cotton cord (140 yards)
- ☐ Two ½" diameter dowels, each 10" long
- ☐ Four 1" diameter wood dowel caps with ½" hole
- ☐ Scissors
- ☐ Tape measure
- ☐ Craft glue

INSTRUCTIONS

1. Glue a dowel cap to the end of each dowel. Cut 34 lengths of cord each 12 feet long; set aside 6 cords. Using lark's head knots, attach 14 cords to each dowel.

2. Lay the leftmost cord horizontally across the cords on one dowel. Working from left to right, tie double half hitch knots around this anchor cord. Repeat this process on the remaining dowel.
3. Using 4 cords for each knot,

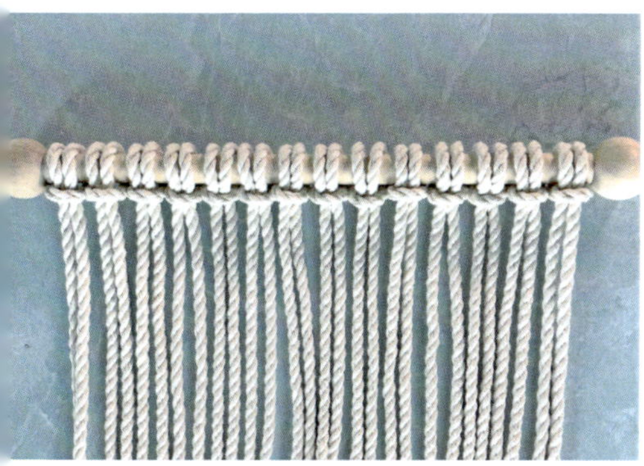

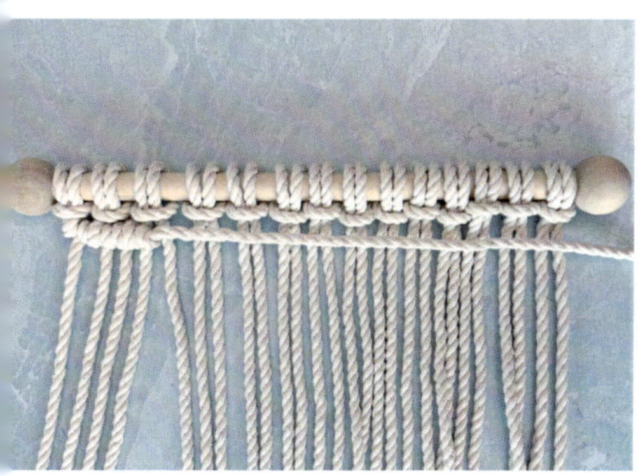

tie 7 square knots across right below the double half hitch knots. Repeat this process on the remaining dowel.

4. Skipping the 2 leftmost cords and the 2 rightmost cords, tie 6 square knots across. Repeat this process on the remaining dowel.

5. Repeat Step 3, creating the alternating square knot pattern.

6. Now we will join the 2 dowel pieces together and begin forming the bag. Tie a square knot with the 2 leftmost cords of one piece and the 2 rightmost cords of the other piece.

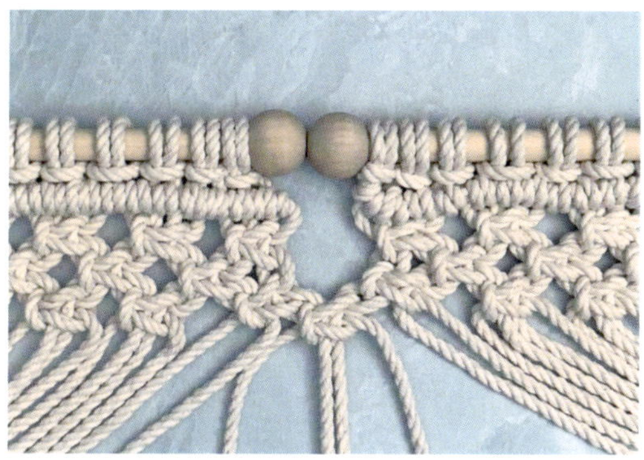

7. Continue tying square knots across until you reach the end and have 2 remaining cords. Tie a square knot with these 2 cords and the 2 leftmost cords on the remaining piece. Continue tying square knots until you reach your starting point. You should have a round of 14 square knots that have joined the 2 dowel pieces.

8. Continue working rounds of alternating square knots until you have a total of 11 rounds of square knots (+ 3 rows of square knots tied in Steps 3-5) or until the bag is about 10" long.

9. The next few rows will be worked on the pieces separately as we form the bottom point of the bag. On one piece, use the 4 leftmost cords and tie a square knot. Continue across the row for a total of 7 square knots. Repeat this process on the other piece.

10. On each bag piece, skip the 2 leftmost cords and the 2 rightmost cords and tie a square knot with the next 4 cords. Continue across the piece for a total of 6 square knots on each piece.

11. Repeat Row 10, but this time skip 4 cords on either side when tying 5 square knots across each piece.

12. Repeat Row 10, but this time skip 6 cords on either side when tying 4 square knots across each piece.

13. Repeat Row 10, but this time skip 8 cords on either side when tying 3 square knots across each piece.

14. Repeat Row 10, but this time skip 10 cords on either side when tying 2 square knots across each piece.

15. Tie a square knot using the 4 center cords on each piece.

16. To join the bottom of the bag, take the leftmost cord on one side of the bag and lay it diagonally along the bag point. Skipping the leftmost cord on the **other** side of the bag, use the cords on the **other** side of the bag to tie double half hitch knots to the bottom point of the bag.

17. Repeat Step 16 laying the rightmost cord diagonally the along the bag point and skipping the rightmost cord on the other piece. At the bottom center point, tie a double half hitch knot with one anchor cord around the other.

18. Now flip the bag over and repeat Steps 16 and 17 on the other side of the bag.

19. Trim the cord ends to 8" and untwist the cords to create fringe.

20. For each strap, use a half hitch knot to attach 3 cords individually to one end of the dowel, placing the cords between the lark's head knots on the dowel and leaving at least a 6" end on each cord.

21. Braid the 3 cords together until the braid is 44" long. Use half hitch knots to attach the individual cords to the other side of the dowel.

22. Finally, tie the cord ends in an overhand knot, trim to 4" and untwist to create fringe.

FAN EARRINGS

You'll have these earrings made in no time–just 3 square knots per hoop! Make several pairs, each a different color!

Design by Brook Berry, creator of BrooklynBerryDesigns.com

Materials

- ☐ 2 40mm metal hoops
- ☐ 2 fishhook earwires
- ☐ Fine cotton yarn (2 yards; I used DMC Natura Just Cotton yarn)
- ☐ Scissors
- ☐ Fine tooth comb
- ☐ Iron
- ☐ Fabric stiffener
- ☐ Clipboard

INSTRUCTIONS (make 2)

1. Cut 4 8" cords. Fold each cord in half and use a lark's head knot to attach it to a metal hoop. Place the hoop under the clip on the clipboard.

2. Using cords 1-4, tie a square knot. Using cords 5-8, tie a square knot.

3. Using cords 3-6, tie a square knot.

4. Comb out the cords with the fine tooth comb. Using an iron, steam and comb until all the loose ends lie straight and flat. Follow the manufacturer's instructions to apply fabric stiffener to the loose ends. Once the ends are completely dry, trim as desired.

5. Attach a fishhook ear wire to the hoop.

RETRO NECKLACE

A perfect twist for the boho girl in you. This simple masterpiece is just a few easy knots.

Design by Lisa Kettell
Finished Size: 1½" x 7½" long pendant

Materials

- ☐ Premade long necklace (I used an antique bronze 30" necklace)
- ☐ 1½" diameter jewelry ring to match necklace
- ☐ 7mm jump ring to match necklace
- ☐ 3mm cotton cord
- ☐ Scissors
- ☐ Needle-nose pliers
- ☐ Tape measure
- ☐ Masking tape

INSTRUCTIONS

1. Cut 6 18" cord lengths. Fold each cord in half and use a lark's head knot to secure it to the jewelry ring. Tape the ring to your work surface.

2. Using the first 4 cords, make 7 half square knots. These knots will twist as you tie them.

3. Using the next 4 cords, make 7 half square knots. These knots will twist as you tie them.

4. Using the last 4 cords, make 7 half square knots. These knots will twist as you tie them.

5. Use needle-nose pliers to twist open the jump ring. Place the pendant and the necklace on the jump ring. Twist the jump ring closed.

ZIGZAG LACE BELT

For a great bohemian look, make this zigzag belt. It only looks hard; the lacy pattern is composed of square knots! Or tie it into a headband!

Design by Janet Von Lone Trieschman

Finished Size: varies

Materials

- ☐ 1.5mm natural cotton cord (yardage varies; see Step 1)
- ☐ Macramé project board
- ☐ T-pins
- ☐ Hair bands (8)

INSTRUCTIONS

1. Decide on the desired length of the finished belt; multiply this length by 3 and add 20" for the tie ends. Cut 8 cords the determined measurement. I cut my cords 134" long for a 38" long belt. Cut 2 36" cords. Tie the 8 long cords together with an overhand knot 10" from one end.

2. Pin the knot to the project board.

3. Take the end of one cord and wrap it around your pinkie and thumb in a figure eight pattern.

4. Remove the wound cord bundle from your hand and place a hair band on it to secure. Wind and secure the remaining cords into bundles in the same manner.

5. Use cords 1-4 to tie a square knot. Use cords 2-5 to tie a square knot just below the first knot. Use cords 3-6 to tie a square knot. Use cords 4-7 to tie a square knot. Use cords 5-8 to tie the 5th square knot. Use cords 1-4 to tie a square knot to the left of the 5th knot just tied. These knots should be on the same plane. This is the zig of the belt design.

6. To create the zag of the belt design, you'll tie square knots in the opposite direction. Using cords 7-4, tie a square knot. Use cords 6-3 to tie a square knot. Use cords 5-2 to tie a square knot. Use cords 4-1 to tie the 5th square knot in the pattern. Use cords 5-8 to tie a square knot to the right of the 5th knot just tied. These knots should be on the same plane.

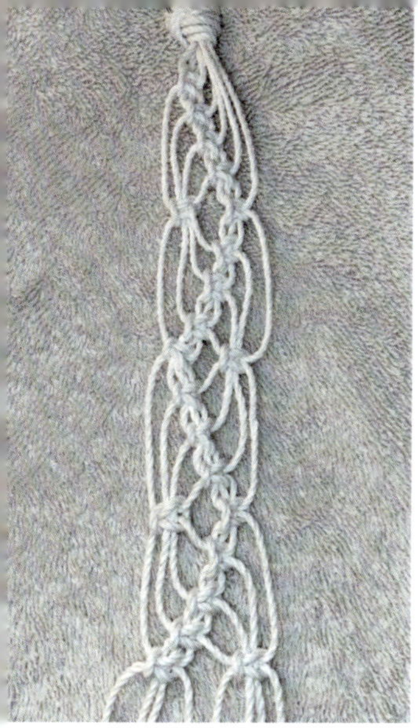

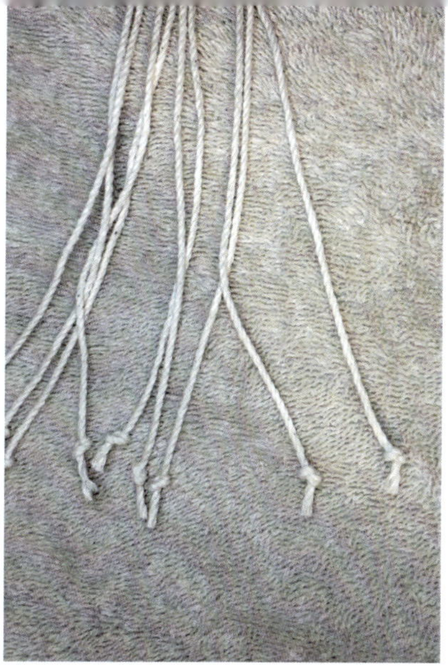

7. Continue this knotting pattern, zigzagging back and forth until the knotted area is the length you decided on in Step 1 and ending with two square knots side by side.

8. Use a 36" cord to tie a wrapped knot around the 8 cords about 1½"-2" below the last pair of square knots. Trim the short cord from the top of the wrapped knot. Or tie an overhand knot as I did on the belt to the right.

9. Trim the cord ends as desired and tie an overhand at the end of each cord.

10. Unpin the belt from the project board. Untie the beginning overhand knot. Repeat Steps 8 and 9 to finish this end of the belt.

11. To accentuate the lace appearance of the belt, grasp each pair of side by side knots and gently pull them away from each other.

FEATHER ACCESSORY

Make this fashionable accessory in your color of choice, since cotton yarn is available in many hues. Or make lots of feathers in lots of colors and tie them onto a swag for your bedroom wall.

Design by Brooke Berry, creator of BrooklynBerryDesigns.com
Finished Size: 4" x 7"

Materials

- ☐ Fine cotton yarn (about 7 yards per feather; I used DMC Natura Just Cotton yarn)
- ☐ Scissors
- ☐ Fine tooth comb
- ☐ Masking tape
- ☐ Split ring key ring

INSTRUCTIONS

1. Cut a 15" cord and 40 6" cords. Fold the long cord in half and tape down the loop (shown on a dowel in the photos).

2. The cords taped to the work surface are the filler cords. Take a 6" cord length and fold it in half; this is Loop A. Place the folded cord under the filler cords with the loop to the left.

3. Fold a second 6" cord length in half; this is Loop B. Feed the loop side of B through Loop A, coming up from the bottom and laying Loop B on the filler cords.

4. Pull the ends of Loop A through Loop B.

5. Pull the ends of both A and B to tighten the knot. This completes the first knot. Slide the knot toward the top of the filler cords.

6. Repeat Steps 2-5, this time placing Loop A with the loop to the right and Loop B with the loop to the left. Slide the knot up to touch the previous knot. Continue tying alternating square knots onto the filler cords until the knotted area is about 3"-4" long, sliding each knot into position on the working cords.

7. Comb out the cords with a fine tooth comb. Using a fabric steamer or household iron, steam the loose ends and comb out the threads. Repeat until the threads are straight and lie flat. Comb the ends down to form a feather shape. Using sharp scissors, trim the ends into a feather shape. Attach the split ring and enjoy!

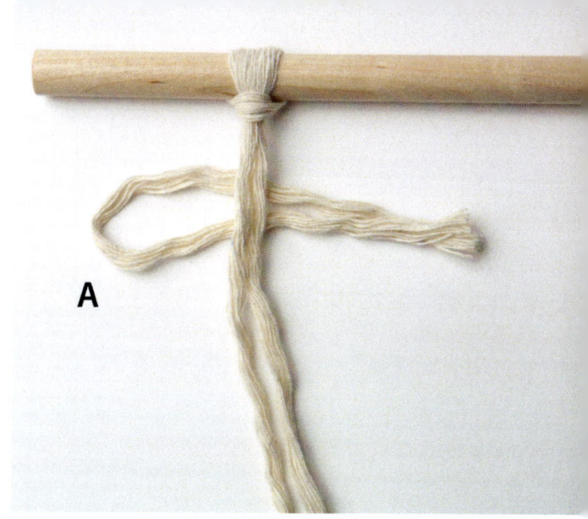

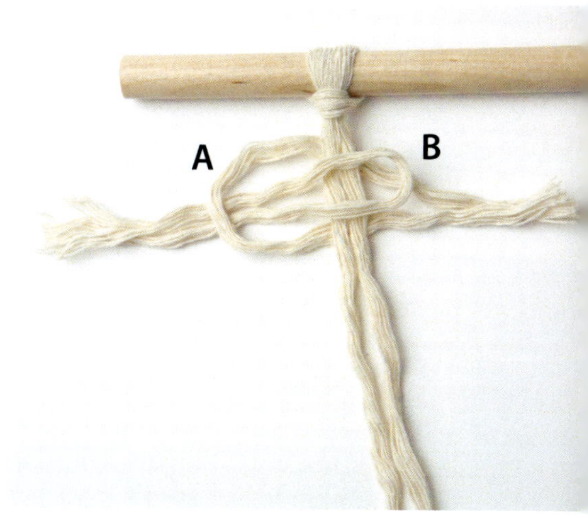

KEY CHAINS

Taping the key ring to your work surface will make knot tying easier.

Designs by Angie Holden

Finished Size: 2"-3½" long, excluding ring and fringe

Materials

- ☐ 1.5mm cotton rope cord (about 8 yards total for all 3 styles)
- ☐ 25mm split ring key rings
- ☐ 3 8mm round beads for Key Chain #1
- ☐ Wool roving or embroidery floss for Key Chain #2
- ☐ 2 8mm round beads and 2 14mm tube beads for Key Chain #3
- ☐ Scissors
- ☐ Tape measure
- ☐ Masking tape

KEY CHAIN #1 INSTRUCTIONS

1. Cut 2 30" cord lengths. Holding both cords together, fold them in half and use a lark's head knot to secure the cords to a key ring.
2. Tie 8 half square knots. These knots will twist as you tie them. String 3 round beads on the 2 middle cords.
3. Tie 8 more half square knots.
4. Cut a 12" cord length. Use this cord to tie a wrapped knot below the half square knots. Trim the cords to the desired length and fray the ends.

KEY CHAIN #2 INSTRUCTIONS

1. Cut 2 30" cord lengths. Fold each cord in half and use a lark's head knot to secure it to a key ring. Tie 4 square knots. Working in a figure 8 shape, weave about ½" of embroidery floss around the cords. Tie 4 more square knots.

2. Working in a figure 8 shape, weave about ½" of another color of embroidery floss around the cords. Tie 4 more square knots. Make an overhand knot just below the square knots. Trim the cords to the desired length and fray the ends.

You can change the order of the weaving and square knots for a different look. Or weaving roving into the key chain for ¾" instead of using embroidery floss.

KEY CHAIN #3 INSTRUCTIONS

1. Cut 4 30" cord lengths. Fold each cord in half and use a lark's head knot to secure it to a key ring.

2. Starting on the left and working toward the center, tie double half hitch knots in a diagonal line until you reach the 5th cord. You will use the outermost left cord as the anchor or filling cord for all 4 knots. Tie 3 rows of double half hitch knots. Repeat on the right side of the key chain.

3. Join the 2 center cords with a double half hitch knot. String 2 round beads on the 2 center cords; string the tube beads on the 2nd cord in from each side.

4. Repeat Step 2 to work 3 more rows of diagonal double half hitch knots on each side of the key chain.

5. Join the 2 center cords with a double half hitch knot. Trim the cords to the desired length and fray the ends.

Decorative Objects

ORNAMENT COVER

Watch the light and shadow play off this pretty hanging bauble.

Design by Olga Boccagno
Finished Size: 3" diameter

Materials

- ☐ 3" diameter plastic ball ornament
- ☐ 1mm nylon cord (about 27 yards)
- ☐ Clear craft glue
- ☐ Scissors
- ☐ Tape measure

INSTRUCTIONS

1. Cut 20 36" cords. Lay a 36" cord on your work surface. Fold 10 36" cords in half and use lark's head knots to attach them to the longer cord. Wrap the long cord around the ornament top and secure with an overhand knot. Choose a cord and use it as the anchor or filling cord to tie 2 double half hitch knots right below the lark's head knots with the next two cords. Attach a 36" cord to the anchor cord with a lark's head knot. Continue tying double half hitch knots and adding 36" cords around the ball. You will have 40 cords now. Separate the cords into 5 groups of 8 cords.

2. Lay the outermost left cord of a group slightly diagonally to the right across the other 7 cords in the group. Starting on the left, tie 3 double half hitch knots diagonally on the anchor cord.

3. Repeat Step 2 to make a second row of double half hitch knots on the left side of the cord group. Make 2 rows of half hitch knots on the right side of the cord group.

4. Tie a square knot with the 4 cords in the middle of the group.

5. Using the 4th and 5th cords as anchor cords, tie 2 rows of double half hitch knots on both the left and right sides of the cord group.
6. Repeat Steps 2-5 with each group of 8 cords. This creates the Petals design, where the knots resemble 4-petal flowers.
7. Cut a 12" cord and tie it around the ornament just below the Petals. This will be the anchor cord. Apply glue to the knot and trim the excess cord.

8. Choose a Petal motif on the ball and use those 8 cords to tie double half hitch knots on the anchor cord, adding an extra loop. Repeat with each Petal motif.

9. Cut 5 24" cords. Attach a cord to the anchor cord in each space between the Petal designs using a lark's head knot with an extra loop on each end. You will have 50 cords now.

10. Make a row of 10 square knots, each using 5 cords.

11. Make another row of 10 square knots, this time alternating between using 6 cords and 4 cords for each knot.

12. Use the right center cord from a 6-cord square knot as the anchor cord and hold it to the right and slightly down. Make 4 double half hitch knots on this anchor cord.

13. Repeat Step 12 with the cords from the 6-cord square knot to the right of the double half hitches just tied.

14. Take the right-most working cord from the 6-cord square knot under the previous row of double half hitch knots. Using this cord as the anchor cord, make a second row of double half hitch knots. Repeat for the cords to the right.

15. Join the 4 middle cords with a square knot braid consisting of 3 square knots. Apply a drop of glue to the bottom square knot in each braid; allow to dry. Trim the cord ends as desired and fray the ends.

16. Repeat Steps 12-15 around the ornament. Tie a square knot with each group of 6 cords that are between the square knot braids.

17. Gather the cords from the square knots tied in Step 16 together; use a wrapped knot to secure them. Trim the cords as desired and fray the ends.

18. Trim the cords as desired and fray the ends, creating a tassel.

MASON JARS

Mason jars have become a standard in home decorating. Take them up a notch by adding some knotted collars.

Designs by Angie Holden

Materials

- ☐ 1.5mm cotton rope cord
  - Standard Mouth Pint Jar - 50 yards
  - Wide Mouth Pint Jar - 65 yards
  - Standard Mouth Quart Jar - 60 yards
  - Wide Mouth Quart Jar - 75 yards
- ☐ Mason jar
- ☐ Scissors
- ☐ Tape measure

MASON JAR INSTRUCTIONS

1. Refer to the table below to cut the appropriate lengths of cord for your jar. All designs use the same lengths.

Jar Type & Size	Cut Lengths
Standard Mouth Pint Jar	47 lengths 36" each 1 length 48"
Wide Mouth Pint Jar	59 lengths 36" each 1 length 54"
Standard Mouth Quart Jar	47 lengths 42" each 1 length 54"
Wide Mouth Quart Jar	59 lengths 42" each 1 length 60"

2. Fold each short cord in half and use a lark's head knot to attach it to the longer cord.

3. Wrap the long cord around the lip of the mason jar and secure with a knot.

4. Adjust the shorter cords so that they are evenly spaced around the jar.

DESIGN #1 INSTRUCTIONS

1. Make a row of square knots all the way around the jar. This is Row 1.

2. For Row 2, make 2 square knots and skip 4 cords. Repeat this pattern around the jar.
   For Row 3, make 1 square knot and skip 8 cords. Repeat this pattern around the jar.
   Repeat Row 3 and then Row 2 around the jar.

3. Gather 2 cords from a square knot and the 2 adjacent cords from the next square knot; tie an overhand knot. Repeat this pattern around the jar.

4. Trim the cords to the desired length and fray the ends.

DESIGN #2 INSTRUCTIONS

1. Make a row of square knots all the way around the jar about ¾" below the lark's head knots. This is Row 1.

2. Using 2 cords from a square knot and the 2 adjacent cords from the next square knot, tie a square knot about ¾" below Row 1. Repeat this pattern around the jar. Continue to make alternating rows of square knots, placing each row about ¾" below the previous row, until you are happy with the length.

3. Gather 8 cords and tie an overhand knot. Repeat this pattern around the jar. Trim the cords to the desired length and fray the ends.

DESIGN #3 INSTRUCTIONS

1. Use 6 cords to tie double half hitch knots in a diagonal line until you reach the 7th cord. You will use the outermost left cord of the 6 as the anchor or filling cord for all 5 knots. Tie 3 rows of double half hitch knots. Repeat with the next 6 cords.

2. Join the 2 center cords with a double half hitch knot.

3. Continue around the jar, repeating Steps 1 and 2 until all cords are used. Repeat Steps 1 and 2 around the jar to make a second group of diagonal double half hitch knots rows right below the previous rows. Tie each knot group to the adjacent knot with a double half hitch.

4. Trim the cords to the desired length and fray the ends.

MEET THE DESIGNERS

BROOKE BERRY

Brooke Berry is an interior designer, maker, DIYer, and the creative force behind BrooklynBerryDesigns.com. She loves to learn new skills and building methods. Her 4 sons believe she can make anything, from installing flooring to building furniture, or even custom shirts! Brooke lives in Calgary, Alberta, Canada.

OLGA BOCCAGO

Olga is a stay-at-home mom of two and a freelance web designer from Atlanta, Georgia. Her first experience with macramé goes back to her childhood. When she was ten, she got sick and spent a week in bed. Miserably bored, her mom brought her a library book about macramé; her first project was a bookmark. Somehow it turned out looking like an ugly owl, but she still loved it and hung it above her bed.

Many years later she couldn't think of a subject for her web design course project. Her teacher suggested to make a website about something she loved to do and wanted to share with others; she immediately thought about macramé. She started posting her works and free tutorials on her website olgasmacrame.com. She's happy to be able to help others in making beautiful macramé items.

ANGIE HOLDEN

Angie Holden is a published author, blogger, and craft lover from Tennessee. While she loves her Cricut, you can also find her doing a wide variety of crafts including macramé. This wife, mom, and grandma loves making and gifting handmade items as well. Want more ideas from Angie? You can find her blog and craft videos at The Country Chic Cottage.

LYNDA KANASE

Lynda is the Creative Director/Designer for i-crafter, a company built by crafters, for crafters. They believe that creating should be a joyful celebration of the imagination and her designs are simple tools to help others discover their creative spirit.

With a degree in Graphic Design, Lynda has designed packaging and advertising for corporations. But as an artist, her passion is crafting, including scrapbooking, quilting, and macramé. Check out i-crafter.com for her latest designs and follow her creative adventures at LyndaCreates.com or on Facebook at Lynda Kanase Fan Club, where you can find fresh ideas and tutorials to celebrate your imagination.

LISA KETTELL

Lisa Kettell is a graduate of Caldwell College, BA and MBA. She has become a leading expert in the creative arts industry and has been published in over 250 publications worldwide. Lisa has taught close to 1,000 workshops, spoken at over 65 venues and has dedicated time to marketing the essentials of art awareness. She proudly wears many hats: graphic artist/illustrator, media platform specialist, branding redeveloper, and creative director. These hats have allowed Lisa to work with over 100 creative industry brands to date. For more info visit her website: www.lisakettell.com

KALEEN LOUNSBURY

Kaleen Lounsbury lives in Des Moines, Iowa, with her boyfriend and three cats. When she's not crafting something up, she's probably tending to her 100+ house plants. More of Kaleen's designs can be found on Instagram at @kbmacrame.

ALEXIS MIDDLETON

Alexis first learned to crochet when she was nine years old with her great-grandmother Persia, and her grandmother Lou. Years later, when she was pregnant with her first child, she was searching for a new hobby and picked up a crochet book at a craft store and has been crocheting and crafting ever since. She decided to name her blog, PersiaLou.com, after the two women who taught her how to hook. Aside from parenting her three children, Alexis loves musical theater, reading, dark chocolate, nerdy board games, and traveling with her family.

DEBBIE MURRAY AND SHEA FRAGOSO

Debbie Murray and Shea Fragoso are the mother/daughter design team behind the lifestyle brand A Gilded Life™. For years, their friends and customers have been referring to them as "The Gilded Girls". Creating their signature romantic art, jewelry, and home décor projects remains their passion and their life's work. The duo can often be found in the dusty warehouses of vintage businesses, curating the offerings of their studio and procuring rare treasures for their website. Other days will find them collaborating on new designs, and dreaming up their next online workshop!
Visit the website: www.TheGildedGirls.com and community: www.GildedGirlsCraftSociety.com

JANET VON LONE TRIESCHMAN

Janet Van Lone Trieschman nowadays is a stay-at-home mom who loves to create. She left a prosperous career as a college professor teaching graphic design to raise her family. Looking for a creative outlet, Janet started a website: Try it - Like it - Create it.
Janet has had a number of articles and reviews published, as well as many exhibitions and honors to her record and has been listed in Who's Who of Emerging Leaders, Who's Who in American Education, Who's Who in American Women, and Who's Who in America.

FaveCrafts is one of the 50 free cooking and crafting websites in the Prime Publishing community. FaveCrafts features thousands of free craft projects, tutorials, tips, articles, giveaways, and more. Their free, daily email newsletter, *Quick & Crafty*, offers crafters inspiration with easy-to-follow projects, tutorials, and gorgeous photos. Every issue includes a variety of crafts including crochet, scrapbooking, kids' crafts, sewing, quilting, knitting…and so much more! FaveCrafts caters to crafters of all skill levels from those just starting out to those who have been crafting for decades.

They are proud of the relationships they've built with hundreds of crafters and companies from around the world and are dedicated to bringing the best content to their loyal and dedicated fans.

FaveCrafts has an active social media community with 500,000 Facebook fans, 282,000 Pinterest followers, and 14,000 Instagram followers. This online community allows crafters from all over the world to share what they're working on and receive feedback on their current projects. Crafters also have the opportunity to be published by submitting their original projects and images to the website. With more than 50 new articles added to the site each week, there's no shortage of content for the crafting enthusiast to explore.

Library of Congress Control Number: 2020900532

Production Team: Graphic Designer – Katie Cooper-Bussell; Photostylist – Lori Wenger; Photographer – Jason Masters.

Made in U.S.A.